Soul Journey of a Yogi Bus Driver

*Stories, realisations
and observations of life
being Soul Conscious*

Simon Ralph

eternalpointoflight.com

This book is both inspired by,
and dedicated to,
my Spiritual Father Shiv Baba.

Thank You for finding
me once again.

It is also dedicated
to all souls of the world,
my brothers and sisters,
my fellow actors.

May you wake up to
the truth of
who you really are,
and remember
your greatness.

Some of the name in this
book have been changed
for the privacy of
those involved.

CONTENTS

PART 1

PART 2

PART 3

Foreword

Love is a great power in human life, and this remarkable memoir can be seen as Simon Ralph's lifelong search to feel and share it – first in ways that lead to degradation and loss, and then through the soul-consciousness of the title, through which he finds renewed strength and freedom.

From a kindly but rather awkward boy who kept finding himself in minor forms of trouble, he graduates to a young man repeatedly embracing altered states of consciousness through sex, drugs, music and any other experience that would help him to 'slip outside time'. Even a stomach massage takes him out of the body and gives him a glimpse of the unlimited.

But he becomes more and more at the mercy of his desires, 'raving and misbehaving', until jobs, homes, relationships and money fall away and he ends up 'left in the gutter of my own self-pity'.

"You can't win with those things," he reflects on the drug-induced rushes of love. "It's just another ball and chain around your leg." Even the 'gentle, peaceful detachment from the world' brought by marijuana, which feels in keeping with his own inner nature, makes him lazy and forgetful and trapped in antisocial behaviour.

It is Raja Yoga meditation, which teaches a distinction between soul and body, and the experience of an inner connection with the Divine that puts him back in the driver's seat of his life. It offers him a better road map, gradually liberating him from his desires, dependencies and negative thought patterns, so that self-respect is restored.

"I felt I was making ground at last in understanding the self and taking control of my physical organs, like a good driver steering the bus on the straight and narrow, through storms of negativity," he writes. "By separating the being from its actions, I am able to remain as a detached observer...and can become free from the influence of situations or people."

Simon has a chatty, friendly writing style and he tells the story of his decline and fall – "I felt sex was very much part of me, if not all of me... lust governed my life for decades" – with humour, and without self-pity. He intersperses his moving tales of loss with nuggets of spiritual wisdom, until eventually we arrive at a life filled with new meaning.

Neville Hodgkinson

Introduction

Being spiritual is not just for religious people. It is not only for the intellectual or learned members of society. Being spiritual is our very nature. It is who we are. We are spiritual beings on a journey through the human experience. Being soul conscious is to understand this concept and to live it. It is approaching life with its adventures and trials, from the understanding that we have come here to learn. We have come to this planet to realise who we are and to learn about the nature of ourselves. It's only when we are in relationship with others, the environment and even our own bodies that this is possible.

It was while working as a bus driver, a service worker that is common to most countries of the world, that I made a few fascinating observations.

It's these ideas and observations, and reflections on them over the last few years, which have bought a series of realisations into my awareness. I noticed that it is possible to compare the relationship between the driver and the bus with the relationship of the soul or spirit and its body.

Through this comparison, I have learned about myself and found many examples to draw conclusions from in order to improve my life. I found that if I wanted to change, firstly I would need to observe the things that I want to change in an objective way. Once I can see the results that my actions and lifestyle will lead to, I am then in a better position to improve the quality of my experience.

This self-observation without judgment takes me out of a 'victim' mentality, which can be extremely limiting. I can then empower myself and increase my self-respect, as well as start moving towards a more fulfilling life and begin to understand my true purpose.

Being soul conscious is a gentle introduction to enjoying our journey as a 'living-light' within this body that we have been given.

I have found that it is helpful to look at our background and growing years to understand some of the reasons why we are the way that we are. Those collective past experiences are useful, but there does come a point when we need to let go of them and move on. When we can let go of the past and learn from it, we can then begin to create our future in this present moment.

Destiny led me through an interesting life, of relationships, exploration and experimentation, before dropping me gently down in the transportation industry. It has been while performing this particular role of a bus driver that many secrets have been revealed to me. Somehow, the opportunity and the freedom of the open road, coupled with the time and space to think and the solitude, crystallised my awareness. The nature of this job is such that there is an opportunity to observe people and life as they pass by, through the windscreen of the bus. A bus driver has plenty of time to think, as his mind can be quite free even while remaining concentrated on the road as he works. It has allowed me the chance of reflection and meditation that was needed to focus my awareness. This awareness brought acceptance, appreciation and gratitude into my being.

A soul-conscious approach to life is the highest gift that I have received and it is my duty to share that gift in any way I can. What follows are some of the lessons that I have learnt along the way.

I have been drawn to embark on writing this book to share with you, the reader, some of the experiences, and observations of this world - all the best bits I have come across on this most beautiful of journeys. Having been lost for many years, or even lifetimes you could say, struggling to make sense or reason of this 'game' that we call life, I was always looking, searching for clues, answers, directions and even guides to show me just 'what' exactly it is I'm supposed to be doing, thinking and being.

I would like to offer my humble observations and ideas about the possibilities and opportunities that we have in leading our lives, only to be of some help, in some small way. At one point, I realised that we can make this physical experience of life a 'dance of happiness and lightness' rather than of survival, drudgery and the mundane. I only wish that someone had handed me a manual about life many years ago so that I could begin to answer the three big questions I have always had.

1) Who am I?

2) Where did I come from?

3) Where am I going?

And of course all the other smaller questions like, Why? How? When? What?

I would just like to say that this knowledge and understanding is not mine, but has been given to me throughout my life by many wise souls and great yogis. They in turn were given this and, as the energy is allowed to flow through humanity, guidance is received. In fact, many of these special people received 'divine' understanding from the 'Supreme Soul', the Father of all souls, directly.

During meditation, I have found that, with connection to the Source of all positivity, I too can experience many elevated states of being. Interesting how I wasn't looking for God or an interaction with the Divine at all, but, quite the opposite, I was just looking for a good time and fun in any way I could, quite literally! It was almost as if I were found, 'playing' in the mud and put back on my feet, brushed down and sent on the path in the right direction. I have no desire to convince anyone of anything. There is simply the thought that every human soul has the right to at least hear ideas and observations of ways that could possibly make their life easier and more enjoyable, even if they don't do anything about it.

Therefore, please don't believe a word you read here, but instead try it out for yourself. Really, that's the only way you will know. Not by listening to me or any (and I mean any) other human being. People have many different opinions and like to 'load' situations in their own flavour in order to gain some sort of small control over someone or something. "Experience is the greatest authority," I have heard it said, so have the experience yourself and the authority received from that experience is the only way you will truly know.

It's as though we all have a 'role' to play, and right now our script says to empty out everything which we keep stored within our mind that is of no value.

Our 'intellect' also needs a good clean out. By this, I mean our conscience, the part of us that knows right from wrong. This is the 'vessel-of-wisdom' inside us that has the power to make the right decision at the right time.

These times that we are living in are crucial to our future. This is a time of 'global transformation'. This begins by firstly transforming ourselves, our lifestyle and our way of living. Also, it's a time of transformation of our environment, the atmosphere and the entire Earth. When we look around us, we can now see signs of change everywhere. The transformation starts here in 'I', the soul, and is then reflected out into the world. As I begin to live my truth, I become positively charged with energy and it affects all those around me. I start to attract others, who are similar, like a magnet and those who want to become similar. This then becomes my nature and influences everything that I come into contact with.

So the wave of energy moves outwards, connected to all those practising similar principles. Like a tsunami of pure and positive power that begins to overlap with others living their lives in an harmonic way, it creates a grid-of-light, linking and growing, which eventually lights up the whole world. This latticework of energy forms a subtle structure that can conduct the 'spiritual light' that God Herself/Himself is constantly radiating (I shall alternate words that denote gender, because the personality of God encompasses all our human definitions).

I see myself as a 'spiritual being' and am sure I have been performing a variety of forms of devotion for many lifetimes. This spirituality crosses all boundaries of religion, race, caste, colour and all man-made borders of invisible division, as well as transcending age, gender and nationality. It connects every soul on this planet as brothers, beyond gender. This bond of brotherhood makes us all children of the one Parent. Please forgive me, as sometimes I struggle to find suitable metaphors or examples to explain a non-physical concept, but maybe you are catching the drift?

The Butterfly

This story shows me the impact that our vibrations and attitude have on the environment around us and on nature itself. It is a true story, which happened when I was visiting a healer named Rita. She was a German lady, middle-aged, whom I had heard about whilst living in the Algarve, Portugal.

There was a group of us - New Age types mainly, dreadlocks, tie-dye travellers, that sort of thing - who were interested in a spiritual healing, a 're-birthing' session to be specific. We arrived early at the typically traditional Portuguese farm house and a little later Rita arrived and met us at her front door. We all stood apprehensively, enjoying the beautiful morning sunshine in the garden in front of her whitewashed bougainvillea-covered house and, as she searched through her bag for her door key, she radiated lightness and positivity, as only an 'earth mother' can.

As she pulled out her keys, a huge colourful butterfly delicately wove in and out of the group, as if it were dancing on a calm warm wind, and caught everyone's attention. Rita giggled with delight and seemed to communicate with the whole of nature. The movement of the butterfly was entrancing and all eyes were on this most delicate of creatures, fluttering effortlessly by.

To our amazement, it gently and very purposefully landed on Rita's finger. I was transfixed by the vibrant colour of its wings as it flapped them a few times, seeming to acknowledge her in a silent communication and then, after a few precious moments, continued gracefully about its business.

Rita smiled in a way that told me that this was not a random isolated incident, but rather a regular occurrence. Such attraction and natural understanding of the nature of energy, as well as life itself, I have never seen since. I labelled her a 'white witch' at that point and this was very much confirmed to me as the healing process continued throughout the day, but more about that later.

Soul Consciousness

So what exactly do we mean by 'soul consciousness'? Basically, it's like turning your entire outlook on life upside down, or maybe the right way up.

We are used to thinking that we are human beings, bodies walking around doing our 'stuff', and so we live life in this awareness. This is fine, but we can then tend to over-identify with everything associated with the body. We think that this is 'mine' and that it is these 'things' that make me, me.

Then what can happen is that those things that define me as being me, for example my job, my husband/wife, my money, my house, my child, can change. Or, worse still, can be taken away. The result of this over-identification, with any temporary roles that I am playing or possession that I may have, is a feeling of 'loss'. The ultimate loss of all being the loss of my own body. This is a fear of the end of 'me'.

Well, it seems a bit pointless to me that death is the end. Or even, in fact, that those temporary things such as name, age, job, home or family define who I really am. This could be quite a limited point of view from which to approach life and you can see how 'fear' then comes into the picture. This is the fear of losing me or part of me, until finally all of me is lost.

'Unstable' is a word that I could use to describe that way of approaching life. 'Body consciousness' is the term we can use to refer to this awareness or way of living.

When we are looking at exactly who 'I' am, we can use the example of a living body and a corpse to understand, by means of contrast. What is the difference between the two? What is it that makes a living body able to move around and perform actions and stops a corpse from doing the same? The life force or the 'spirit' or 'soul' is the only difference. One has a soul living inside it and the other does not.

So who am I? If I am the living body, then how much of that can be removed before that body is no longer me, e.g. amputated arms and legs, liver transplant, heart transplant etc. These days, with machines, a body can be kept alive for quite some time, but it is not conscious, e.g. in the case of a coma. It is the 'consciousness' that holds the personality, memory and awareness. In the case of coma, it is often reported that the 'living being' is aware of what is going on around its body in the hospital, but is unable to respond, as it seems to be trapped or separated or disconnected from its body, while somehow still remaining connected to it.

It's like thinking that I am the bus that I drive...! When really, I know that I am the driver. The bus cannot move without its driver, unless other machines are used. The driver is the one in charge of the bus and is needed to move it. In the same way, I am the driver of this body. I am not the body, but the energy or entity that is moving it. Without the driver of this body, the body is just a corpse and completely useless. In the same way, the bus is useless without its driver. They both need each other.

You could even say that the body itself is 'non-living' and just organic matter, without consciousness, without its driver, the soul.

This is how it feels to me, "I am the spirit, or soul, and the feeling is that I am sitting within this body, looking out." The same way that the driver looks out of the windows of his bus.

The body can be compared to the bus (which is big) and 'I', the tiny soul, am the one who is sitting in the driving seat, driving it.

A few other metaphors may help to explain this concept.

1) The Pilot and the Aeroplane - The plane cannot fly without the pilot, in the same way that the body cannot work without the soul.

2) The Musician and the Instrument - The instrument (body) cannot produce a sound until the musician (soul) plays it.

3) The Hotel and the Guests - A hotel is empty and lifeless without any guests.

So, the feeling changes to that of being a 'guest' within this body and in that way I feel that I should look after this body. A guest looks after all the things that she uses, although they actually belong to someone else. She then becomes a 'trustee' of those possessions or that property and takes special care so as not to damage anything; otherwise she will have to pay a price in some form or other at some stage. She doesn't own the things she is a trustee of and, if they do get broken or lost or damaged, she doesn't feel as if she has lost anything. She can be quite detached about this, not uncaring but carefree, and find that she can look after things even better in this way. She uses everything carefully and with respect and responsibility.

In the same way, I should be looking after the bus, my body. Without the bus (body), the driver (soul) is redundant. Without the body, the soul has nowhere to sit and no vehicle to move around in or instrument to play through and express itself in the physical world, through its senses. With this awareness, it becomes my responsibility to look after the body carefully and to use it with regard and love, whilst all the time knowing that 'I', the driver, am more than just that body.

The body, which is limited by time and space and is only available for a temporary period as part, and only part, of my overall journey, is now very valuable and precious. It becomes my friend and I start to love it, no matter what society, the media or advertisements try to tell me about the way it should look. After all, what is normal? Normal is the conditioning and expectations of society, and is often connected to consumerism and how we can best be manipulated to consume more goods that we do not really need in order for others to gain profit.

PART 1

THE BEGINNING

The beginning is always a good place to start. A beginning is a very delicate time. This applies to all beginnings.

When a baby is born and is beginning its life, it is very delicate. When a flower first sprouts from the ground, it is also soft and delicate. Both are precious and valuable, and need great care and attention. They need to be nurtured and encouraged in order to give them a chance in this world and for the best to be brought out in them. The baby needs love and caring, it needs food and warmth. The flower needs sunlight, water and protection from the elements.

An idea, plan or project is also delicate in its beginning.

When a business is beginning or being developed and is growing, there is a delicate period while services or products are being created and presented. As the staff members are being trained and the concepts promoted or products refined, times are delicate. As ideas and systems become stable, the business begins to receive credibility, respect is earned and a reputation is built.

The early years of a child are delicate. This is the time that many habits and personality traits are created. Ideas and standards, values and virtues are also established in these days at the beginning. As children, we are very much influenced by our surroundings and the social structure that we are brought up in.

The beginning is the foundation on which we build our lives. That is not to say that the beginning will ultimately shape our future, no! It will however colour our initial approach and attitude to living.

The first part of this book looks at some of the events and situations that shaped my present. It looks at how circumstances and synchronicity led me to where I am now. There were a few powerful episodes that influenced the beginning of my journey towards self-soul realisation. These episodes highlighted to me the impact that people, places and events can have on the state of our awareness while we are beginning to walk the path of life.

Greenwich Community Centre

Greenwich Community Centre is where I received my introduction to 'Raja Yoga Meditation'.

It was the beginning of a new way of life, which I have now been practising for over 14 years, and 'woke' me up to the realisation of being a soul.

The Centre just happens to be close to where I was living at the time and where I was attending Iyengar Yoga classes. Iyengar Yoga is a set of postures (exercises) that, when practised regularly, are said to give flexibility to the body, and health and longevity to the lifespan.

It also happens to be about three miles away from the place where I had left London, to travel around the world some 12 years earlier in order to seek my fortune and find myself. This drama of life is strange like that; I feel that nothing is a coincidence. There are always hidden secrets and signposts along the way, if we are only aware enough to catch or notice them.

My partner, Hanna, and I enjoyed Iyengar Yoga, and would practise in the Greenwich Community Centre twice a week. One day she saw a leaflet saying 'Learn to Meditate For Free'. This 'free' meditation just so happened to take place in the very room next door to our yoga class and we decided to try it out. After all, it was free.

"Nothing to lose," I thought. Little did I know that I would in fact lose everything, everything negative that is.

The following Wednesday evening, we decided to go along and have a look. This worked out perfectly, because the Iyengar Yoga classes were on a Tuesday and Thursday.

The room in which the meditation was taking place was pretty basic and the facilities simple, to say the least. It consisted of a circle of rickety old plastic chairs in the middle of a dreary small hall with high ceilings, that was a bit tatty and looked like it needed a good lick of paint, and with a table in the corner. The room was lit with neon strip lights, which were quite harsh. The music came from an old tape recorder that played squeaky old cassette tapes that whirred and clattered, due to their age and being stretched and distorted out of shape with use.

The meditation group consisted of about ten people, with a 70%/30% ratio of Asian-Western, all fifty and upward. I think I was the youngest person in the room at thirty three with the eldest reaching maybe seventy five. The format was of some talking and guided meditation commentaries, which led the group into a meditation experience. It seemed to be aimed at beginners as well as intermediates, which I liked.

The person who was speaking, and seemed to be running the session, was an older lady from Ghana, who was bubbly and warm with a kind smile and very gentle but firm nature. I found out later that her name was Ada and she was in her 60s. Her vibration was very calm, sweet and 'matter of fact'.

We all introduced ourselves and she began to explain the idea of the Raja Yoga Meditation, which we were about to practise, and how it is useful for relaxation and practical for everyday life. "It removes stress and also helps others with whom we come into contact, like friends, family and colleagues," she shared. She explained that, "It's when I change, that the world around me changes."

"That seems to make sense to me," I thought.

Ada started to guide the group into the first meditation and set off the squeaky tape cassette player with some peaceful, yet 'low-fi', music.

"Strange," I thought, "this doesn't seem to be a very relaxing environment," as the strip lights glared in my eyes and my buttocks rested uncomfortably on the hard plastic surface of the 1980's-style school chair.

Unexpectedly quickly, I completely forgot about my buttocks and the room's limitations, as Ada began to take us into an inner journey of discovery. I don't remember quite what she said; it was something about the original nature and qualities of the soul, and I don't really know how long it lasted, but I do know that the experience was life changing.

She inspired us to, "Just follow the words and let go." Let go I did, but following the words was not so easy, especially as the walls of the room were becoming less and less solid, and starting to change colour. This distracted me a little, but in a nice way. From grubby white and stained, with a few cobwebs they began to turn subtle pastel colours of yellow, green and blue, then to pink, to orange and soft red.

"Nice," I thought. It was as though, somehow, someone was throwing cans of subtle paint all over them, similar to an artist's palette for mixing the required tones and shades of a masterpiece. The depth of field within the room started to change in my vision and the magnificent, beautifully coloured walls began to breathe in and out, in and out.

"Lovely," I thought and, feeling very safe and secure, I enjoyed the feeling of continuing to let go. I allowed Ada's sweet words to drift past me, through me, over me and inside me.

Now I was unaware of anyone else in the room, I began to melt or 'merge' as the room seemed to fill with light. Not light coming from the strip light, but gentle pulsing light that didn't seem to have a source. The room became so full of light, and a wonderful vibration of love and peace, that I just let go completely and spun into a world of harmony, tranquillity and perfect balance.

I seemed to be very distant from the place I had started, gliding free into an unending sky of golden light. It was as if my consciousness or awareness melted into the experience of truth. This truth cut through all logic of thoughts and thinking, penetrating my very being and existence; I was flying beyond. It was a feeling of absolute freedom, liberation and delight. That's all I remember. Beyond words, sounds and touch. 'Super-sensuous joy', happiness outside of the realm of the physical senses, is the only way to describe it, and even that is inadequate.

The next thing I knew there was a faint sound in the distance and the words, "…is everybody OK… is everybody OK," began to float in my general direction. Ada's soothing voice continued, "…is everybody back…,"and it wafted into my ear. Suddenly, I realised that these words were directed at me. My eyes opened and I could now see through them, but the rest of the body was paralysed. Everyone in the circle was looking at me, but I was frozen. "Is everybody OK?" she whispered. My awareness seeped slowly through the whole of my head and face, from the warm, radiant glow that came from between my eyes. I began to nod gently, as I could now feel my neck come alive again, but still I was partly detached from the rest of my body.

The energy of the soul was pulsing slowly through the body, filling it with 'life force'; similar to the way a container or vessel gets filled with gas or even a warm liquid. Life and feeling came back to the arms and torso, and gently down into the lower body and feet. It took a few minutes until 'I' was back, but back from where? Everything was soft. The room still looked vibrant and pastel coloured. It was almost as if I was not actually touching the chair that I was sitting on or the ground on which my feet were resting. I was so full of love, lightness, I could hardly respond or talk, or maybe I just didn't want to break the perfection of that moment. I sat there content and satisfied, as well as astonished, while the session continued around me.

Ada gave me a knowing smile, as if to say, "...everything is fine, you're absolutely safe and, yes, I know exactly how you feel."

As the session came to a close, I stood up slowly and, sure enough, I was still floating. There seemed to be no contact with the floor and I felt as if I was walking at one fifth gravity, just like on the moon. This feeling of light and lightness, of love, peace and harmony stayed with me for the whole evening. Later at home, I went to sleep in this same state but, when I woke up the next day, sadly, I was back to normal.

"What on earth was that?" I thought and, "How can I get some more of it?"

But remember, this beautiful experience is not the aim, only a side effect of steps taken towards realisation and enlightenment through meditation.

Background - Living and Learning

Even in the beginning, somehow I always knew that, "Everything would be OK in the end..." How? That I didn't know. But this was the feeling I had from the age of about 6 or 7 years old. As if I had done it all already, many times, and that I just needed to play out each scene as it came along, and that happiness was already guaranteed in the end.

One of the earliest questions that I can remember asking my mother was, "Mum, what happens when you die? Where do you go?" Only the blissful innocence of a 7-year-old child could deliver such a profound question and actually expect it to be answered. It was as though I already knew the answer, but had forgotten, and that I needed to be reminded of it. With an open mind and a face full of curiosity, I asked of her to answer this most auspicious of questions. My mother was, and indeed still is, a very kind and generous lady, full of high morals and values. As a practising Catholic, she replied, "...we don't talk about that sort of thing..."

This closed down any further discussion on the matter. It seemed like a good answer, at the time. Of course I don't blame her, she was only saying and doing what she thought was best for a normal, infant school child. But, I was never normal.

'Average' was a word often used in labelling Simon throughout his school days, "...just below average and can do better, an under-achiever," that kind of thing. So this was the role that Simon took on, accepting what others said as truth, being conditioned on some sub-conscious level. As sure as eggs are eggs, he never did quite fit in and, boy oh boy, he tried.

His upbringing was caring, safe and simple. There was plenty of love within the family, with the normal stuff like fighting with his younger sister Kath over the TV remote control. It had only just been invented and consisted of four buttons of supreme power – two to change up and down for the channel and two to change the volume, just up and down!! Advanced, Hi-Tech living for those times, and a must-have for all forward-thinking households.

Still, the family unit functioned the way it did in the 1980s. The family would all have breakfast together sitting at a round dining table in the extension of the semi-detached house in Redford Avenue, which was situated in a conservative Sussex market town called Horsham. There was one of those 1970s lampshades, that was over-sized and round, made of mesh, with a kind of resin or glue in the holes, that was great fun to pick out with your finger nails. Almost as satisfying as when you pop the little bubbles in a big sheet of bubble wrap, but not quite. Same sort of feel though.

Toast and cereal, chat and school, Simon having begrudgingly just completed his gruelling morning newspaper round. You know, that sort of thing.

Simon seemed to be quite popular at school. He was in many clubs and sports teams, thinking that was 'fun'. He was neither bright nor dull. He enjoying science and maths, but was hopeless at English. In fact, reading was his main 'issue' at school. It just didn't seem to make any sense, wasn't interesting or fun, and actually brought great anxiety, stress and fear, just at the thought of it, which was actually able to physically and mentally paralyse him. 'Terror' was the word he would use to describe the thought of reading out loud and he would do everything in his power to avoid this 'fate worse than death'.

Tuesdays and Wednesdays were English days, 'doubles' both days. Yuk, he hated and dreaded it. As the class worked through the register by surname alphabetically, each one reading their bit, darkness would descend on him as the time got closer and closer for his slot. He would become near hysterical, beginning to sweat and hyperventilate, then experiencing distress and faintness. These were the physical experiences of repulsion he would become familiar with during those school days!

These moments felt like a form of medieval torture, as he desperately tried to get the words out. He would try to prepare himself by reading ahead of the class before his turn came around, practising the part that he thought would be his piece, guessing and hoping that that would be the right part. Practising over and over, longing to get it right, trying to save the embarrassment and pain. Then it would finally be his go.

This blocked energy within expressed itself as a panic, close to vomiting. It was an intense distress, with disruption to the breathing. Palpitations and long, ...pauses... "HELP!" He just wanted to, "run...anywhere.... somewhere away from here!" It was as if the words were stuck, sharp, compressing his throat and lungs, painfully being squeezed out, not dissimilar to a dose of constipation, with every other word being filled in by the teacher or his best mate, or some other kid, which was even worse.

Time stood still, frozen, or even reversed itself, in some twisted form of trickery. The ordeal would continue for maybe one and a half pages of extreme tension before the teacher would say, "Well done," but Simon knew it wasn't...

Finally, after what seemed like an eternity, another student would take over. "Safe...," well for another week anyway... These were, all in all, dark moments. They were moments of horror, frustration, self-criticism and doubt.

As you can imagine, this experience had a devastating effect on his confidence and self-esteem, and stayed with him for many years to come. Indeed, shaping his very future and holding him back from many possibilities and opportunities. Narrowing down options and squashing any interest in being 'at the front' or 'on show' or having to speak or read in public - worst case scenario!

After going through this ordeal, I am not only extremely aware not to damage any person in this manner, but I also realise that it had to be that way for Simon.

I feel now that it was probably the return of some actions that I may have performed in a previous lifetime, which had to be repaid or played out as settlement. This is often known as karma or karmic accounts, but we'll talk about that more later.

Being a 'fat kid', as you will know well, if you are or were a fat kid, is not easy! Kids can be so harsh and I mean really nasty, downright spiteful and, more often than not, it's the fat kid that gets the brunt of it.

Genetics were not on Simon's side at that young age - bit spotty, tall but chubby, he, as with many young people, hated his body. Too big in some places, too small in others, out of proportion, funny-looking. He could never find any shoes or clothes to fit. However, it turned out that this worked in his favour as he gave up on fashion and image early on, so freeing himself from that avenue of desire and distraction.

Now, all this said, Simon was still a happy boy, always riding his bike or kicking a football around, trying to keep away from the 'bullies'.

The summers were long and everything was taken care of. Although the family was always a bit tight for money, he wanted for nothing.

"Money doesn't grow on trees, son," his Dad would tell him. Maybe this was also a kind of subtle conditioning or programming on some level which indeed affected him for decades. There didn't seem to be much of it about, but somehow it never had any 'value or meaning' or made any sense. It was more of an inconvenience.

For many years later on in life, I lived on a shoestring-budget of 'just enough', preferring to have time and space rather than money and things.

There were a few teenage or adolescent incidents of impact and influence that coloured Simon's upbringing. The first major one was connected with 'bullies' and violence.

"It all started in the park where we would play football, the 'Rec' or recreation ground, near home, when some older, scary looking boys began to disrupt our game. Rumour had it that these were the glue-sniffers that used to hang out in those parts! There was a stand-off, and the usual antagonism and name-calling moved on to shouting and intimidation.

As we retreated out of the park to safety, I found myself unexpectedly holding a stick in my hand as some sort of automatic defence system. Unusual, as I wasn't a violent or angry child in any way, but for some reason I had picked up a small stick that day."

The incident moved on, from verbal abuse and threats, to missile throwing. You know, cans, sand, grit and even stones between the two gangs. It was at this point that I performed an action (karma) that I would regret for years to come. You guessed it, I threw that stick in the general direction of the other boys! I don't know why, it just happened like that... And then I ran."

Can you believe it? It actually hit one of them! I mean, what were the chances (synchronicity) of that actually happening?!

"There was a scream, and I ran and ran not even looking back to see what had happened, panting, heart pounding with fear and remorse. A sense of deep regret and disbelief descended upon me over the next few hours, worried beyond imagination and in a state of dismay as to what had taken place.

Distraught and horrified, I later found out that the 'fateful' stick had hit one of the other gang members in the eye. Well, not actually in the eye, but just under the eye."

This was what was reported anyway. True? Well, I'm not sure."

"The grief and guilt were too much and, as they set in, I was filled with and experienced, hopelessness, blaming myself for everything so badly, that on some level I knew that I was in great debt to this boy for nearly blinding him."

Although, really it was probably more like just a scratch.

"I detested my behaviour and wished that I could turn back time.

The saga continued. Being in the same school and one year older, he 'played' on my guilt through endless bullying and harassment in the coming years. As it was my fault (in my mind), I allowed the bullying to go on, without fighting back, trying to 'pay off' the action I had taken. It was as though I needed him to be able to hurt me as much as I thought that I had hurt him. The 'accounts' needed to be balanced and, until they were, I just took it."

This was my first awareness of 'karma' and I just could not understand it. I felt like a coward, scared to fight, scared to cause any more sorrow to that soul. This was very confusing and very difficult for a young boy to understand, or any adult for that matter. But this universal law had taken over and was in control of me in a weird kind of way.

"It took 3 or 4 years until I felt that the accounts were clear internally, by which time I had taken many 'batterings' and much ridicule. By this time I was growing fast, physically, and many hours at the local gym after school had made me muscular and strong. I think he realised that he had better not push his luck any more. The karmic account had finished. So it naturally reached its end without confrontation from my side."

Somehow Simon would always find himself attracted to the underdogs or dropouts, maybe subconsciously he could relate to them more than everyone else, feeling their pain. He felt sorry for them, wanted to help them, those ones who didn't fit in, just like him. This magnetism caused him to stay in 'dodgy company' much of the time and influenced both his friendships and education in a negative way.

One best mate had a few psychological problems. Another, at the age of 17, began to 'rob' banks with a starting pistol and would make his getaway on foot, later starring on 'Crime Watch UK', a TV programme about criminals caught on closed circuit TV in the mid-

'80s. Another friend later committed suicide by hanging himself on a very specific type tree. He had been a cabinet maker prior to that.

Later, Simon somehow ended up in a group that liked to drink lots of beer and get into fights and up to general mischief wherever they found themselves, but fighting was never his preference. After a year or two of Friday nights out with these characters, and lads' holidays which inevitably ended in tears, normally his, he realised that brawling and pain were not his idea of a good time. Broken bones taught him that there must be another way to resolve conflict that didn't hurt so much!

A Broken Nose

Thus, this beginning was my introduction to realising the effect of my words on others and how they then in turn affect me. I learnt this lesson in a very practical, as well as painful, manner! This happened in the 3rd year at secondary school, aged maybe 13. And, man, it hurt like mad.

I was coming down a stairway in one of the school buildings at Tanbridge House Secondary Modern School, which consisted of an old fashioned main house dating back to early 1900's, from where the school was governed by the Head and a collection of cranky old teachers, and a collection of prefabricated post-war out-buildings in which the learning took place. This was set in beautiful playing fields on the edge of the commuter-belt town of Horsham. Incidentally it has now, to my horror, been converted into a residential estate and a Sainsbury's supermarket. Well, at least they kept the grand main house, which still brings back memories of savage 'rollockings' from the Head Master in his musty study when I occasionally pass by it! 'Authority' never was my idea of fun.

As I passed one of the 4th form boys, he needlessly let out a barrage of abuse, swearing at me for no apparent reason, concluding by referring to me as a 'C###'. I stupidly reacted by swearing straight back at him without thinking. After all, I was getting more confident in my old age of becoming a teenager and it just seemed the appropriate thing to do at the time. This he didn't like at all as he was amongst his class mates, and was not receiving the respect that he felt he deserved.

The next thing I knew was PAIN.

SMACK! He punched me right on the nose. It was so hard that I couldn't feel the whole of my face. There was just a cracking sound and the fuzziness from the impact of his fist.

I was shocked, "This had never happened before!!" I was stunned and off-balance, then WHACK another punch in the same place. This one caused my nose to explode with an avalanche of blood, but strangely it didn't hurt as much as the first one. I really saw stars spinning around my head, just like you do in cartoons.

I remained standing, but in shock, pouring with blood. It was the first nosebleed I had ever had and it was like a cascading fountain. Tears streaming now, I felt totally alone and disorientated. I wasn't angry, but more surprised and stumbled around trying to find this boy, not to hit him, but more to show him what he had done.

Well, it turned out that I had been in the wrong place and said the wrong thing to the wrong guy at the wrong time. He was a boxer!

The story continued after I came out of hospital, where they had to reset my nose. The experience in hospital was interesting, apart from when I came around after the anaesthetic and found that I had about 10 metres of bandage stuffed up each nostril!

The nurse said that it would be fine, as long as I didn't sneeze. That night in hospital, while I was asleep, I sneezed and the bandages shot out of my nose like bullets, wrapping themselves around me, caked with blood and crusts, while still attached to the inside of each nostril. Imagine being woken up by that. It looked like The Texas Chainsaw Massacre (an '80s 18-certificate horror movie which I had luckily managed to watch, aged 11, with my mate, Rich, and his chain-smoking, liberally-minded Mum from across the road where I lived. We also had the chance to enjoy the full movie range of sex, violence, and depravity of the era in that smoke-filled living room during the winter months). I was wrapped in blood-soaked bandages like a 'The Mummy', another top horror film of those times. This was a terrifying and disturbing way to wake up after such a traumatic episode, I can tell you.

There was talk of prosecuting the boxer from my parents, taking him to court for 'ABH', but, once again, without realising it, I accepted my karma and took it no further, feeling that I must have had to pay for something that I had done before. I had a real deep awareness of finishing the situation there and then, and not dragging it on any more. After all, what would that prove?

Now, with spiritual knowledge and awareness I call that putting a full stop, 'past is past', moving on to the next scene. On some subconscious level, I must have known this, even before I learnt the spiritual laws behind it. Strange, how past residual memory is somehow stored deep within the soul. It's a kind of natural feeling, and does make sense on the level of spirit, yet, is far beyond logic or rational thinking.

At the time it was all impossible to understand. Like a foreign language in an unknown place, for a marooned sailor on a desert island, struggling to survive and make sense of things.

Discovering Meditation

Meditation saved me from myself. It gave me hope for my future. I was always trying to have some sort of out-of-body experience or another. Some sort of 'altered state'.

Firstly, it was through alcohol. I found this method while I was quite young and had a pretty harsh first lesson with it, once again learning that if I didn't take responsibility for my actions, I could get myself into some deep trouble.

Aged 12 or 13, I can't really remember exactly, I went on my first proper holiday alone, although looking back, I wouldn't call it a holiday, more of an ordeal! (By then I had already been camping with the Swindon Road 2nd Scout Pack many times, but I felt that that didn't really count. It was always fun though, with a good measure of hay fever and sleeping rough in Bivouacs, tents made in Native American Indian style out of branches and leaves under the stars, and eating baked beans off of metal plates with dubiously hygienic cutlery).

This first true adventure away from home alone was a school exchange trip to Spain, the idea behind it of course being to improve the very strange, obscure and complicated language of Spanish. This was the opinion of most students in my class, and probably the reason I was the only one going to Spain from Tanbridge. All the rest of the students on the trip were from neighbouring schools.

Well, I wasn't really having a very nice time in Albacete, south eastern Spain, about 160km from Madrid, while staying with the wealthy family of Ramon, the Spanish exchange student that I was paired up with. It was a mixture of loneliness, boredom and probably homesickness, not to mention the fact that I couldn't speak the 'lingo', that I found myself out one night with some other English students. It seemed like a good idea to have a few beers in the local bars and quite a novelty, actually being served at that age. We were drinking beer out of litre glasses and I'm not exactly sure how many we had, but it was a few.

Then someone suggested that we have shots of a spirit called Anisette that came in a greenish bottle (it's a strong aniseed flavoured 40%+ liqueur) along with the beers. "Fine," I thought. So we had a couple of these 'chasers' and after that the rest was a bit of a blur.

Well, I did remember a few kind-of-dreamy memories from that night, but it was all a bit hazy. Very hazy!

Next thing I know, it's the morning and I'm in my bed, feeling a little disorientated, but ok-ish. This is when I got the full rundown of what had happened. It was a story that I couldn't believe and dismissed immediately, thinking that this was some kind of a joke. That was, until I saw the physical evidence.

Apparently, I had spent the night in hospital, after the mother of the family who were looking after me had found me passed out, eyes dilated, in my room, with a very, very slow heartbeat. Can you imagine how she must have felt? She must have thought I was dead or something!

Poor lady. Especially as she was the one who was supposed to be responsible for me!

I don't know how I got there or what I had been up to that night! As I was told the full details, I really thought that, "OK, the joke has gone far enough now," and I was beginning to get upset, as a teenager can, when they don't get their own way.

When I looked down at my arm, there was a gash running the whole length of my forearm and it felt quite raw. This, I was told, happened in the hospital, when the doctors were trying to hold me down while giving me an injection of adrenalin or something to try to speed up my heartbeat, and I lashed out just as they put the needle in. The syringe tore a long cut down the entire forearm….ouch!

If it hadn't been for the mother's quick thinking and actions to get medical help, they told me, I may not have ever woken up from that night. And, if it hadn't been for the gash in my arm, I would never have believed a word of it. That is the 'power' of the effect that alcohol can have on our awareness or consciousness. I had been unconscious of all events the previous night, yet was still able to function, walk around, well stagger probably, and even get home, yet unable to remember a thing.

This unconsciousness reminds me of the way that we are living our lives at this time, as if we are sleepwalking. I also see that it's not our fault, but it is the result of living from a body-conscious perspective for a long time and this is where it has led us (being soul conscious is the antidote).

Worrying! This incident put me right off drink for a few years and, even now, the smell of aniseed makes me retch! Not sure what happened that night, but I think that, if I were a cat, I would have used up most of my 9 lives. It's amazing how deeply unaware you can become whilst drunk and yet still stand up. I could have done anything that night and been none the wiser. This is similar to the current condition of the soul, absolutely unconscious of itself, yet still functioning.

This is the contrast that I felt after first finding out about meditation. It was as if I had been walking around asleep for 33 years, like a zombie with zero awareness, then 'Bingo', I woke up. This was my conclusion as I first felt the experience of being soul conscious through Raja Yoga Meditation.

Whether this was chance or synchronicity, it was hard to say at the time. But looking back, I am now able to see the Divine design of the events leading up to that first flight of the soul. Meditation can be very much like flying. It is this feeling of lightness that was, and indeed still is, most attractive.

It also came at a time when I had almost given up on life. Having been married, divorced and with one child, I had tried everything I could to find answers to my many internal questions and a reason to live. "What's the point?" I thought. I'd tried travelling and had been on the move, on and off, for 12 years or so. I travelled through over 40 countries, searching, looking for 'clues' or answers to the questions that people not only couldn't help me with, but also couldn't even understand why I was asking in the first place!

Europe, Americas, Australia, Asia. No luck, just emptiness and loneliness, sorrow and hopelessness. There was a 'twinkle' in India in the early '90s, but, at that time, I was still sleepwalking, stumbling around the world, unaware, stuck in the depth of body consciousness and at the mercy of my own desires.

Relationships, high adventure on the oceans, trekking in the Himalayas, dangerous sports, sex, drugs and rock 'n roll, well 'house music' anyway, raving and misbehaving, as they used to say!! Still, no joy or, if there was, it was short-lived and limited. Like Mick Jagger said, "I can't get no... satisfaction..." And trust me, "I tried."

Part of that search took me into the world of music and with that came drugs. I became lost in a hedonistic trip of music and narcotics, of highs and lows. Whether it was pills or powder, dots and 'shrooms', hash and grass, whatever, it just didn't matter. Ten years passed me by in the blink of an eye. Each day, and that's every day, consisted of getting 'stoned' or high...or both.

Lost, lost...lost! It was part of 'The Search', now focused internally with mind-altering substances.

Introversion? Well, kind of! Not the extroversion of the years spent in world travel, but dependence on substances to take away the pain of the mundane and shallowness of this limited reality which I found myself in. There was a particular preference or persuasion towards psychedelic drugs and the way they altered perception and increased awareness of other dimensions. They seemed to take me part of the journey towards spirit. It took me ages to work out that, although they did open up the mind a little, they left me empty and in pieces, with even more questions than I had started off with. They often took me to the 'destination' without the map to get there or, indeed, to get back and gave no understanding or reward in the process.

I became fearless with the dosages, only wanting to go farther than the last time, without regard for the self or others. This was a true sign that it was time to STOP!

Towards the end, there were a few encounters with darkness or dark forces and I am sure this was exactly what was needed to transform this most destructive of hobbies that I had chosen. Or maybe had chosen me?

Libido...

In the early years and at the beginning of my teens, I remained quite innocent. That is, until the urges of puberty began. From then on, sex and my desire for it were always insatiable. I just could not seem to have too much of it. These uncontrollable energies can take over our thoughts, words and actions, and shape our attitudes, intentions and motivation. This was very much my experience.

After the initial sexual obsession had worn off (this took about 10 years), I searched for some magic entrance though the 'tantric doorway' into a world of enlightenment, but really I was just fuelling my desires and becoming trapped in dependency. I made the same mistakes in each relationship, which then played out with one girlfriend after another, repeating old habits just with different partners in a different set of circumstances. What a loser!

The drive for understanding reality overtook me. After 5 years of marriage, my wife, Tami, and I were gradually growing apart when our daughter, Ella, arrived. Tami stayed another year and then she left.

This was extremely painful at the time, but I don't blame her, after all I was out of control and prepared to sacrifice all for a taste of truth.

I used to think, "What I need is a guide, someone to show me just what it is I'm supposed to be doing here!" I had become obsessed with knowing what life was for.

Everything was being stripped away from me. Friends started to avoid me, thinking that I had 'lost the plot'. Work had no significance. Money had no value and possessions were irrelevant.

"I must be here for more than just existing, struggling and surviving?" I thought. "Why am I here on this planet, now?" was always ringing in my ears, along with tinnitus from listening to extremely load music over a long period of time!

My family didn't understand me either, but always remained supportive and for that I am extremely grateful.

Jobs and money disappeared. It was as if my identity, or the one I thought was mine, just crumbled away. I began to feel vulnerable and almost 'naked', left in the gutter of my own self-pity.

I was lost in this dark period for almost 2 years, living a very simple life in a rural part of southern Portugal near Faro, the airport town of The Algarve. However, a kind of caterpillar-type transformation was taking place. On the outside, there was relative stillness, clutching at new ways of being and expressing, while inside, fuelled by a series of New Age books and interactions with the international, 'alternative' people of the Algarve, rapid development was occurring. My consciousness was awakening. It was just that old habits, and mostly negative ones at that, were still ruling the soul.

A few minor illnesses erupted during this stage. Kind of a clearing or cleansing process, I suppose. One of which led me to the psychic lady named Rita. It was through her that I first met the 'Divine', but, strangely, not in the form I would have imagined. Rita was, without doubt, a 'white witch'.

Re-Birthing – Chakras

Chakras are the 'energy vortexes' that are located in and around the body, and I had very little understanding about them at the beginning of my spiritual journey, with no actual experience or knowledge. In time, I found out that they are spinning discs of light/energy that form part of our energetic structure.

This visit to the healer was connected to a health issue. The suggested treatment was a stomach massage and both Hanna, my girlfriend, and I were to receive this at the same time, during the session. Yes, I was a bit sceptical but also interested as I had been working with energy already in my own way without too much guidance for a few years already, and had begun to tap into some strange experiences.

So together, in a small, first floor flat, in the rather New Age town of Lagos in Portugal, we tried out this most fascinating healing technique.

Rita, our German friend, spoke very little English and had been practising this type of 'circular massage' at the stomach region, around the stomach chakra, for a few years, but I had the feeling that she had never before quite experienced what was about to happen.

We lay down on a blanket on the floor, head supported on a cushion a metre apart and Rita began to massage our stomachs each in turn. Hanna was first for about 15 minutes and then it was my turn. I have to say, this was a new experience for me and, at first, I was a little self-conscious as she rubbed massage oil in a circular, spiral-type motion around my diaphragm, stomach and lower abdomen. It was in no way sexual, but extremely sensual and sensitive.

The stomach area began to heat up with the friction of her hands and I began to feel a woozy sensation, which continued until I felt almost sick. As I relaxed into the firm but gentle sensation of heat, movement and pressure, I began to become disorientated and felt quite 'sea-sick'. My sense of balance was completely lost. The massage became relentless as it continued and the heat in that area built up so much that I no longer felt the contact of Rita's hand on my stomach. It was just a ball of heat, which felt slightly outside of time, if that makes any sense.

On and on, she continued to knead, press and manipulate the knots and energetic blockages, opening this area up, giving an elastic quality to the midriff. She worked in the way a potter moulds a clay pot from its raw elements to its finished article, with love and attention to every detail. She was deeply focused, with intense concentration, as she radiated positive energy.

The feeling of 'falling' and 'spinning' increased through my awareness. Heat and pressure, cycling and circling. I began to lose track of what was happening, in a way that was not dissimilar to becoming drunk or feeling a drug being metabolised within the body. I was losing consciousness. I struggled mildly for a few seconds before 'surrendering' to the experience and, in a second, the awareness of my body dissolved.

I melted, somehow being sucked into a whirlpool of energy that engulfed my being and was centred within my stomach region. I fell into this spinning, energy vortex, which is really the only way I can describe it.

As I fell into my own stomach chakra, I became separate from the body and, in fact, the body was gone, it had disappeared and was now nowhere to be seen. I was outside of it, or above it, or somewhere, but definitely the body had nothing to do with me. I was soaring through an 'astral plane' of some sort, completely free and beyond the physical world, in a chaotic place of images, shapes and colours, but of no physical form. It was quite abstract and I was absolutely without fear. I had become free and fearless and had moved away from the physical dimension, unconcerned about my body. As if I had never even had a body in the first place and so had no worry about its safety or even its existence. I could not define what or who I was, and had no connection with sight, sound or touch. The physical senses did not exist, but I still had a perception or a viewpoint, only it was vast and seemingly limitless. Movement and space were there, but depth and any form of gravity had been removed.

I was being propelled through an unknown location. Within or without, I really cannot say. Geometric forms and obscure images flashed by me in a weightless, timeless, dimension of light and haze, until I became aware of a large 'Isosceles Triangle' (that's the triangle with two sides of the same length and one, in this case the base, a shorter length) standing in the distance.

Strangely and without words, for there was no sound, I called this form towards me in thought and it came into the middle distance. It was a huge, transparent, stable, towering triangular shape. Amazed at the ability to influence or encourage this 'entity' to move, within this seemingly chaotic soup of estranged elements, I tried again. I called this magnificent being again with a thought form like a silent scream, and it moved ever closer and towered above me (whatever 'me' was) right up close like a translucent skyscraper. It was almost transparent, extremely powerful, huge and stable.

I wanted it; I desired it with a deep feeling of recognition and love, like a child needing a hug from his parents. I called it one last time towards me. It obeyed my wish and crashed right through me, like a plate glass window smashing into a billion pieces. It was fantastic.

Suddenly this frantic yet subtle world of strangeness became completely still and calm. There was dead silence. Peace. Unlimited peace. Divine peace. A stillness that I had never known could possibly exist. There was absolute calmness and peace of a quality that connected me to God Himself. Light, unending love and intense happiness, bliss. Stunning.

This was enlightenment in a second and it was timeless. There was an instant sense of knowing. Knowing 'everything' at once! It was such a contrast to the journey through the treatment of the massage, which had been a bit bumpy to say the least for it had consisted of muscular spasms, involuntary convulsions and contracting of the reflex movement, similar to a new-born baby (if you have ever seen a baby's 'startle reflex', you will know what I mean. It's when the entire spine and limbs react to a sudden interaction, and is one of the most basic and primary reactions a human being can have). There had also been floods of emotion, washing through and being expressed in the form of tears and cries. At one point, there had been shouting and screaming, which I later realised had come from my body. As the soul regurgitated past memories and acted them out through the body, I was unaware of performing these blood-curdling cries and primal screaming until I was shocked back into consciousness by hearing them through my ears, only then realising that they were coming out of the mouth of this body. This was a little shocking and jolted me during the massage process, disturbing the flow of treatment. Rita had pacified me and reassured me in such a way that she was able to continue with her work.

Endless peace and upliftment permeated my being. It felt like a complete revelation of overwhelming relief. This was the result of the energy work.

I had caught a glimpse of the non-physical for the first time, without using any external catalysts. The opening of the stomach chakra had triggered it all. I realised that we are 'energy'. Energy is what we are made of. Pure energy.

Later, with the help of a German translator, Rita shared her experience of the events that had taken place. To my amazement, she had seen exactly what I had seen. It was as if she had accompanied me into this other world and had been a guide for me as well as an observer.

Maybe she had seen more than I, as she gave me great regard after that day. She said that I was 'global' in my awareness and that the Algarve and Portugal were too small for me. I had no idea what she meant.

This was a glimpse into the unlimited and the beginning of my relationship with the 'Supreme Energy' or 'Supreme Soul', although it took me another 6 years to work that out!

The Search

What is your purpose? Is it to accumulate wealth or to procreate? Is it to eat, drink and be merry? Is it to wake up every day and go to work? Is it to be grumpy and chase pennies? Is it to survive another week in the rat race?

Why are we here? What is it that we are supposed to be doing? What's it all for anyway?

I don't know about you, but this sort of 'chatter' always used to be running through my mind. Sometimes louder and sometimes quieter, depending on my level of contentment, but always still there, even in the happiest of moments.

Driven by an uncontrollable desire to answer some of these questions, I began travelling the big wide world thinking that the grass would be greener on the other side, wherever the other side was! And of course, it wasn't. The same emptiness and loneliness followed me around as if it were a ball and chain around my leg.

Even a paradise beach, that is always so enticing on the posters in the window of a travel agent, would seem insufficient and unsatisfying, and I would be looking around trying to work out what was next. Which drink to have or food to eat or pill to take or person to meet?

This continued for a few years. I just couldn't put my finger on whatever it was that I was looking for, that always seemed to be just over the horizon. Whenever I got there, it was just another mirage.

Over the years, there were a few pivotal points when 'shifts' seemed to happen. These shifts of awareness would normally happen after standing back from situations and reflecting on the way things are. Then with a little time and space to ponder, coupled with a moment of clarity and a very determined thought as to which fork in the road to take, change would materialise.

After all, 'change' is the only definite thing!

Vocation

One of these moments of clarity spurred a longing to find my vocation, the beginning of which uprooted me once again from my surroundings and repositioned my attitude both mentally and physically.

Up until that point, I never really had any direction in my life and was a bit of a wanderer. My focus was constantly moving and changing. I would try one thing for a while, then realise that it wasn't what I wanted and so would try something else. This happened for years with jobs, houses and relationships. The problem is that, when you keep changing, normally you have to start again at the bottom and learn again. Then after a short while you find that, "No, this isn't for me either." Exhausting and non-productive are two ways to describe this.

So I packed up everything that I had, which consisted of a suitcase, a backpack and maybe four boxes of bits-and-bobs and returned to England to try to find myself, again.

This took courage and was a brave move, as it felt like the last chance. I was getting too old to just wander around, and needed direction and an aim. The role that I had been playing and my karma in Portugal was coming to an end and it felt quite natural to go, to move, in order to create something new. I had learnt many lessons in that quiet environment close to nature, but I was becoming stagnant in expression.

Life was passing by and I was going nowhere, and fast. I would have to leave this comfort zone and FACE. Face the things that I had run away from a few years earlier. To let go of a support or comfort zone, even if it was one that didn't bring happiness, and step into the 'abyss' was what was needed and I was ready for it.

Over the years, as I lost interest in places, and even people around me, due to changes in things we had in common, or, the directions in life that we were pursuing. I would find that those scenes of the 'drama' would quite naturally just slip away. Then the thought, "Time to move on....," would come. This was one of those moments.

Direction, vocation, reason were the issues that caused my internal conflict. Nothing seemed to have any value. My inside and my outside did not match - there was imbalance in my actions and my thoughts. I needed to harmonise myself somehow.

I was still looking for answers outside of myself, not realising that I had to look deep inside to find the solution. "Where's my guide?" I would think, "...Where are you...?" I was looking for a person, a human being, to tell me what to do, as we often tend to do. We just give away our 'inner power' and trust somebody else to think for us and direct us according to his or her ideas and ideals. The only snag is that other human beings don't know either; they just think they do and continue to let us down…don't they?

Motivated by purpose and vocation, I was attracted back to England in the way a needle is magnetised by a magnet and unable to resist. After a year or so, and while practising hatha yoga, I stumbled across Raja Yoga Meditation. This was the beginning of a new life, almost as though I was reborn while already in this body. Meditation was the treasure that was waiting to be discovered and, at last, I had found the map.

Cleansing was taking place in those early days. It was like a big clear out or a 'spring-clean'. This was very much highlighted by another amazing experience or gift that I was given. It was a gift that I feel was not for me to keep to myself, but one that would have to be shared.

Laughing and Crying

This cleansing was the beginning of an emotional clear-out that was long overdue and was a very memorable meditation experience. It happened quite soon after I started to practise Raja Yoga. This particular cleansing continued for about a year afterwards as well.

One afternoon, while I was alone at home in the London Docklands apartment that I had unexpectedly scored from a supermarket notice board at a bargain price,(it even had a swimming pool and sauna with a gym, all available to its residents) I sat in a comfortable space next to the window overlooking the Thames, on the floor, cross-legged and began to meditate. I focused on seeing myself as a being of light, as a soul, like a tiny star, sitting at the centre of my forehead.

The lighting in the room was low, and I was positioned in front of a candle and an image of a point of light, radiating light outwards. As I began to slow down the body, releasing it of all tension and heaviness, I became more and more relaxed and was somehow able to turn my attention, my awareness, within.

The room around me seemed to slowly dissolve into insignificance, and I began to connect to myself as light, a being of conscious living-light. The thoughts had slowed down and there was a feeling of freedom, stillness and silence and a warm glowing sensation throughout the body.

Next, from nowhere, the feeling came that 'I', this eternal being of light, and not just this limited physical body, was a child of God. The realisation expanded into one of having been lost for a very long time and now being found once again and in the arms of my Supreme Parent. This relationship, one of the Divine Father/Mother and His/Her child, filled me with happiness and the love flowing from this Source of Power was overwhelming and deeply moving. It was such an intense feeling of being reunited with 'One' after having been lost for so many births. I was reduced to tears and I began to cry involuntarily.

These were not tears of sorrow but 'pearls of joy' that were emerging from my eyes and streaming down my face. Instantly, I became soaked in these waves of love, not only physically but also spiritually. Each new flow of these jewels of water sent an ecstatic feeling of relief and happiness through the body. The energy/light was racing up and down my body, from head to toe, like electric shocks of pure delight. Euphoria increased each time I said internally, "Long lost... but now found..." This phrase continued to be repeated in my mind, over and over again automatically, and lifted me higher and higher, up an unlimited stairway of light and love to a never-ending point of ecstasy.

It was pure delight. There was so much happiness being experienced that my face became contorted and stretched with laughter and an ever-increasing smile that felt like it was turning my whole body inside out.

The intensity continued to increase, tears turned into weeping, weeping into sobs of joy and elation, not dissimilar to the rebirthing session years earlier with Rita. Later, I realised that this was the same Energy that I had met previously in the form of a 'triangle'.

The awareness of the room, the body and anything that our physical senses normally detect did not exist. There was only a crescendo of ever-increasing happiness, relief and overpowering laughter. Higher and higher surfing on the laughter and floods of tears, I was climbing a ladder to heaven. There seemed to be no end to this 'current' that was streaming through me like pulsating light, till it was almost unbearable. I was awash with pure love.

"How much more could there be?"

"How much more can I handle?"

"Will it ever stop?" filled my mind. So much happiness and joy. It was timeless, bodiless and carefree.

Eventually, on a certain arc of this spiral of laughter, there was a switch, or should I say merging, into more weeping and sobs of relief. Every emotion that had ever been suppressed was working its way through me. As if being washed from the inside, soaked and soothed. Everything, which had been held within me for so many years or even lifetimes, was flooding out in a tidal wave of emotion. By now my shirt was so soaking wet with tears that you could have wrung it out. My face was aching from laughter and stretched like elastic. My stomach was compressed from pushing these residual feelings outwards, sides splitting from the laughter, throat open as these forces moved through me and took on the form of physical sound. During these moments, I was unaware of anything except light. After this phase of tears and at a certain point of the spiral, once again a switch or merge seamlessly transformed back into laughter. Howling with laughter, rolling about uncontrollably in stitches of laughter. Non-stop it went on, more and more laughter with tears of joy. On and on and on it went, powered by a connection to an external source of Unlimited Energy. Light and electricity still filling me with constant waves, shifting, massaging and releasing deep blockages caused by discontent built up over decades. It was wonderful.

This 'flip-flop' of weeping and howling with laughter took me to the brink of exhaustion. Drained, as though the body had just completed a triathlon and the soul had been cleansed of unwanted emotions and freed from its suppression, calmness finally arrived.

I really have no idea how long it went on. As the point of total exhaustion was reached, the thought came, "What must my house mates think is going on in here, with all this noise?"

These emotions were cleaning, cleansing and renewing, as the water poured from my eyes. E-motion is energy in motion, i.e. it was moving through from one point to another and it felt so good. This thought marked the end of a most beautiful experience. It took me back into the physical world and trapped me back into body consciousness (fear, worry, concern, conformity) and out of my state of divine delight and soul consciousness.

That experience still seems fresh today and it still feels very real. It feels like a perfect memory, like one coming from the 'days of my childhood'. An idyllic memory.

The DNA of the Soul

To begin with, what is the make-up of the soul?

According to my understanding, the soul is spiritual energy. But what is the mechanism through which it works with the body in the physical world?

Here's an interesting way of looking at it and seeing it from a larger perspective. This is something to reflect on when you have a few spare minutes, maybe in silence or when meditating. Try creating this picture internally as if you are painting an image inside the mind. Use concentration and focus to expand the possibilities within your awareness.

First of all realise that 'this' is not all that there is. I mean that there is more to life than we are aware of with these physical eyes and our other sense organs. For example, have you ever been thinking about someone and then, all of a sudden, that person phones you up?

Somehow we are able, occasionally, to sense events or interactions before they actually happen. This is due to a certain state of mind or of our awareness.

The physical world that we live in seems 'solid', but, in fact, it is just made up of energy or light. Matter is stored energy and is made up of atoms, molecules, protons and neutrons, which are all moving about at different speeds. This speed is its 'vibration', or you could say its 'frequency'. This is what science tells us. However, it looks like it is solid when we see it with our eyes, and we do tend to rely on our sense of sight a little too much.

A blind person cannot see and so can only 'understand' these solid objects with her intellect. Yes she can touch, listen and smell, but the conclusion taken from this information is made internally in her mind. The picture she creates internally may look very different from the picture seen by a person with sight, even though it is the same object. This is because a different mixture of information has been received and processed, giving a slightly different outcome.

Soul conscious vision is the most accurate way of looking at life. It shows us the truth. The truth is that which is permanent, and not just the temporary. The temporary truth is actually only part of the truth and can fool us. Soul conscious vision is more reliable than our physical vision when we are interested in knowing that which is of benefit to us and to others.

You could say that the physical world is a reflection of the inner world. As I think about something, I create a thought and then may, or may not, put that into action within the physical world. This action is performed by the soul, through the body. 'I', the soul, am the creator of my experience. I use my mind to create thoughts. I put those thoughts into actions through the body to fulfil my desires and to get what I want or need.

However, I am not my mind or my thoughts. Rather, I am the creator of my own thinking.

As with the driver of the bus, I, the soul, am driving the mind and, later, the body follows by putting that thought into action. Which direction should I drive the bus; which way should I steer it? Where should I steer my thoughts that are being created within my mind? Remember that I am not my mind, but the driver of my mind.

Where is the mind located?

The mind is non-physical. You can't see it, so where is it located?

The brain is physical and, neurologically speaking, you can see it. It is the 'hardware' that the mind works through, lighting up different parts. The mind, however, is in the soul, and the soul is who 'I' am. The soul is made of non-physical, spiritual energy/light and can never be destroyed. It just changes form. I do not *have* a soul; I *am* a soul. The mind, as well as the body, is part of what makes me a human being.

It's like I am the captain of a ship and the mind is one of the crew members. Ahoy!

Or, you could say that the mind is like a naughty child, getting up to mischief and playing tricks on me.

So, there has been a mutiny on my ship and it's time to take back my command. But how?

Well, the crew have lost their wisdom and are basically doing whatever they like at my expense. Discipline is what is needed. Yes I know, we don't like the sound of that word, but try to see it in another way.

Do it with love.

When these subtle organs of the soul are working *for* me and are co-operative crew members of my ship, then the ship of the soul sails in the right direction, one of contentment and happiness, and everything goes well. We're talking about the soul-self.

All this stuff is going on inside - no wonder everything is getting out of hand. If the people on the bus start to get a bit rowdy, I need to act with authority. I need to be firm but fair and resolve any issues in a non-violent manner. I find it helps to get the other passengers involved as well, as it adds wholeness to the solution when there is unity and co-operation.

Sensitivity and reason are my non-violent weapons and I need to use them as a great warrior uses his sword and shield. For this, I enlist another crew member, my intellect, which, at this time, has fallen asleep on the deck as no-one is listening to him.

I need to empower my intellect, so it can have the authority to take action, and discipline my mind with love and guide it in the right direction. I need to start to create positive thoughts, which will then go into action through the body. All of this happens in a split second, at the speed of light, which is of course, what the soul is made of. Non-physical light.

How do I empower the intellect and make it my co-operative worker? I really need it to be on my side and become my friend, and to make friends with my mind. It's when I can become objective and not judge these two crew members that I can retrain them in a loving manner so they can help me. After all, I would rather not have them be my enemies. We need to sail across this ocean of life on the high seas of adventure together, as a team.

When I'm meditating, I speak to myself like this internally and find that I can easily develop a good relationship with these two subtle organs of the soul - the mind and intellect. It's like a running commentary between two of the parts of me, and I'm the one overseeing it.

The job of the mind is to create. That's what it does. It just creates thoughts, more and more of them. It doesn't care what type of thoughts, it just manufactures them in the same way that a factory makes its products.

If the mind is not my friend, it starts to become unhelpful in its production of thoughts, often creating wasteful or negative thoughts that can spiral in a downward motion and cause me distress.

To check the quality of my thinking, there needs to be the 'quality control department'. This you could say is my wisdom and it is located within a container, in the part of me called the 'intellect'. Not as in 'intellectual', more as in my decision-making ability or my power to decide. It is the power to know right from wrong, up from down, left from right. The job of the intellect is to verify each thought before putting it into action through the body, and so creating a habit. My actions, through my body, then become my personality and so my character.

When I can encourage both mind and intellect to work together in harmony, I can experience benefit for myself. This is the principle behind the method of my meditation. This inner dialogue leads the mind into a positive creation and a pleasant experience for the soul-self.

Meditation
– Qualities of the Soul

The following commentary is exactly how I speak to myself internally, slowing down my thoughts and reaching a place of silence. I do not try to stop thinking.

Raja Yoga Meditation is active, not passive. I guide my thoughts in the direction that I want them to go, like the bus travelling along the road in the right direction.

It's useful to practise this type of reflection each day and it only takes about 10 minutes. Even quicker, once you get the hang of it. I keep my eyes open when practising my meditation. This makes it very practical and easy to bring into my everyday life. I allow my eyes to rest on a point ahead of me and I turn my attention inside.

Sitting quietly, I slow down my body.

I ask my mind and intellect to check the body for tension and tightness - they obey with co-operation and my attention goes to each part willingly.

I scan through, from toes to head, and let go.

Relaxing my feet...feeling the pressure release, I allow them to become loose and free.

The intellect moves its focus up through the legs, together with my mind's eye, my attention, and I (the soul) let go of any stress in the calves, thighs and the back of the legs...

Moving up through the torso, releasing any tightness from the stomach, lower back and sides....

Continuing upwards, letting the chest and upper back become loose and relaxed...

The arms are allowed to be soft and free, the hands and fingers easy...

I bring my awareness up through the shoulders and neck, loose...

By now, the mind and intellect are working together in harmony as a team, with my guidance.

Up to the jaw... relaxed... the face... soft... the skin... eyes... and cheeks, free from tension...

The head relaxed and easy...

Now, with this awareness, consciousness, that has been checking the body, move to a location at the forehead, between the eyes, and focus a small ball of light in this place.

Feel a warmth or softness, as if the sun or a warm wind is gently shining or blowing on the forehead.

Now, just as I have slowed down the body and brought it under control, I can turn to the mind and begin to slow it down...and begin to focus it in the way you would an old-fashioned camera.

Slowing down my thinking, I let go of the past, just for a few moments... I let go of the future, just for a few moments… putting down anything that has to be done - I can deal with that later…

I come into the present moment…

The present is a gift…

Creating space inside the mind…

Space between the thoughts…

If any unwanted thoughts enter the mind (the intellect quality-checks each thought for its benefit), I give them zero energy and watch them dissolve like clouds in the sunshine as they pass me by.

I have created some room, some space, internally.

In this space, I ask the intellect to guide the mind and I can now place a very powerful thought…

I am a beautiful being of light…

The intellect gives this thought the go-ahead and the mind begins to expand it.

I am a sparkling, shining star, like a tiny point of light, at the centre of my forehead, radiating pure light outwards…

The intellect checks for any unwanted thoughts. I check my concentration and my focus…

I am a peaceful soul… full of peace… overflowing with peace and light…

Again the intellect agrees and the mind continues to increase this train of thought.

Peace is all that I am, nothing but peace, showering peace outwards… and I fill with that peace…

I am a loving being; full of love… showering love into the atmosphere… I don't need to ask for love… I am Love…

I am a pure and powerful soul, full of happiness and wisdom…

The mind/intellect team are now working together seamlessly.

I know exactly what to do and when to do it, and exactly what to say and when to say it…

Easy… happy… and light…

I, the soul-self, watch or observe this feeling and experience and enjoy it for as long as I want, checking where my mind is and remaining present, in the now. As this practice begins, the intellect becomes stronger and is able to gently guide the mind, which, of course, keeps running off and playing in the dirt like a small child.

With attention and a little time and love, the intellect holds the hand of the mind. They become great friends and play together. The mind then creates positive thoughts with the help of the intellect. Then the soul gives the go-ahead and, as the 'king of the self' seated on his throne, puts them into action through the body.

Now, the 'captain' is back in control, at the helm of the ship. The bus driver is back on the right route, travelling in the right direction of life once again.

Our Habits

Have you got any?

Maybe you pick your nose at traffic lights or maybe you don't replace the toilet roll when it runs out so the next person gets into trouble if they're not careful! Or maybe even worse than these two examples!

Would you like to know how to change your habits?

As we begin to understand ourselves, and become a detached observer of the self and our subtle organs, we are able to start to change our habits.

Do you want the map?

Habits are made of repeated actions or even non-actions. When the habit is repeated, it becomes stronger. It gets loaded with feelings, memories and sensations. It eventually becomes part of our personality and is stored as a record within the soul, i.e. me. These traits and preferences become a 'tendency' within us. The 'recordings' become strong through repetition of action and are stored within the soul as an imprint. This then shapes our responses and reactions, and thus the way that we play our part.

Once the thought has been created and checked for its quality and benefit, it is put into action through the body and a memory of it is recorded in the third of these internal, subtle elements of the soul. We can call this third element of the soul the 'sanskars'. This is a Hindi word that sums up more than the words habit, trait and preference, and so is best not to translate as its meaning is much more complete.

Sanskars are like a filing system and, as the action is continually repeated, the file gets bigger and stronger and more influential. It's like an imprint or groove, subtly sculptured within the soul. Inside the sanskar of each action is recorded the feeling, experience and memory of that action. These sanskars or habits become our natural response to an event and make up our personality. They make us the way we are and, in many ways, define us. Our habits or sanskars can then be triggered as a reaction by situations or people and express themselves instantly though the body without any thought taking place. Often this happens without being quality-checked by the intellect.

This can be a problem, as the sanskars are now controlling my responses and may well be giving me a negative experience, without any wisdom being activated. Therefore, I become a slave to my habits. Not good.

When all these subtle elements inside 'me' are working together with me, life becomes easy and sweet, smooth and effortless. The trick is to get all three of them on your side, rather than have them against you!

How can we do this?

Well, meditation empowers the intellect and gives it the strength to make a good decision about the quality of each thought and then only allows the beneficial thoughts to be put into action, so creating positive sanskars. This then reinforces future thoughts and actions, so making those positive, beneficial sanskars strong. The intellect then begins to have the strength to reject any harmful thought patterns, which may be destructive to the soul in some way.

As I focus my consciousness on the beneficial, it expands and becomes bigger, so giving me the experience of those beneficial thoughts in real life. In this way, I don't even need to look at the negative, it just naturally becomes small as the positive grows and pushes it out of my awareness. This is the method to change our personality, because our deeply ingrained habits become our character.

"Watch your thoughts; they become your words,

Watch your words; they become your actions,

Watch your actions; they become your habits,

Watch your habits; they become your character,

And watch your character; for it becomes your destiny."

Frank Outlaw

Whatever goes in
will come out

The way that we live our lives has a massive impact on our consciousness and this affects the experience that we have in life. When we begin to observe just exactly what we put into our bodies, we can improve what we get out of life.

For example, the food that we put into our bodies affects our behaviour and the quality of the thoughts we produce. Look what happens when children eat too many sweets; they can become hyperactive and uncontrollable. You can almost see the sugar being metabolised as their behaviour becomes frantic and chaotic. They lose concentration, the speed of their mind increases and their actions are carried out at double speed.

Food additives can do the same, as well as cause dependency. At one point, I developed an addiction to cans of soft drink and eventually experienced a fungus type infection on my tongue. Even that didn't stop me from consuming 2 or 3 cans every day. Luckily, I realised that it was becoming unhealthy and stopped the habit.

Heavy foods can make us sleepy, as the body diverts energy to digest them; blood is needed in the stomach area, so leaving the brain a little short of oxygen. It's quite likely that the soul sits in the centre of the brain, maybe at a point called the hypothalamus. From there, it can control the body and all its systems. When the brain is a bit short of oxygen, due to digestion taking place, it slows down and the consciousness or awareness can become slack. That's why we sometimes nod off after a heavy lunch on a Sunday.

Lighter food is more balanced for the body and so doesn't impact the soul as much, which means that we can stay more alert and focused. You can see how the body and soul work together as a 'team'. Each needs the other in order for us to function as human beings.

A vegetarian diet can be useful in order to facilitate more gentle thoughts, which are in line with the natural flow of nature. Whereas, a non-vegetarian diet can produce aggressive thoughts, which could have some relationship to the vibrations/energy stored in the animal's flesh such as fear and anxiety at the time the animal is slaughtered. Remember energy cannot be destroyed; it just changes form as it is transferred. My question to myself at one stage was, "Do I really want to ingest that sort of energy?" As I began to realise that food energy, when ingested, can manifest through my own thoughts, words and actions, I really had to look at this seriously. At first, my ego fought against it.

An even subtler concept is the way I prepare my food. The consciousness and my frame of mind can affect the vibration of the food that I am preparing to eat. If I am cheerful and happy, my food will be charged with that energy. If I am angry or sad, the vibration will attach itself to the food in a similar way. In this way, I check my thoughts as I am making my own food, sending light and love into it as I prepare it. Do you know what? It even actually tastes nicer and becomes a pleasure to make. It's just a switch of awareness; it's just being soul conscious during food preparation.

In fact, everything that I put into my body, including the information that I see, hear, touch and smell, has an impact on my mind. If I want to become the 'master' of my own mind and make it my friend and not my enemy, I will need to treat it well, with respect, and take precautions as to what I put in it! Otherwise, it will continue to run around like that naughty child, playing tricks on me and behaving mischievously.

Can you imagine the effect that TV has on my mind?

If I watch violence on television, it begins to create violent thoughts within my mind over time. These thoughts then become my words and eventually I may put them into action, all because I saw it first on the TV and thought that, "It's OK, I can handle it, it won't affect me." It's a form of subtle negative programming, and maybe not so subtle either. Other media can do the same if we allow it to.

How can I discern what is true and what is false? What is fiction and what is real life when the 10 o'clock News shows scenes of disaster around the world, followed by a disaster movie? Our 'power to discriminate' between truth and falsehood becomes diluted and distorted.

I've heard it said that, on seeing an angry person, the memory remains as an imprint for six months. Every time I see that the person, the memory of that anger is triggered and the associated feelings are linked between the two. So, best to be cautious as to what you feed your body and mind, as they are easily influenced.

Ego – Body Consciousness

Let's begin by defining what we mean by ego in this context. Ego is the limited 'I' of approaching my life from the perspective of being (only) a body. This approach and limited understanding of my true identity is a huge misunderstanding and is the root of many problems.

When I identify with being only the body, I tend to create a false image of myself based on the way that I look, the things that I do and the temporary ideas that I use to define myself.

All of these ideas can be taken away from me in a second, leaving me 'stranded' and in a state of despair about myself.

This can happen when a person is made redundant from her job for example. If she has over-identified with that job and it is taken away from her, she can experience deep loss, not only of income, but also of identity, value and self-worth, thinking that part of her has gone. Really, she is the one playing that part or role and it was not who she fundamentally is.

Here are a few examples of how we can feel depending on our perspective or our viewpoint of the world, ourselves and our experience in life. These contrasting feelings were noted, and shared with me by a mentor, and highlighted to me the vast differences of a life approached from these two states of consciousness.

When I am in body consciousness: -

- I feel anxious and uptight

- I am grumpy and short-tempered

- I can turn my friends into enemies

- I am out of harmony with my body

- I can waste time, energy and money by being indecisive

- I have too many expectations of others and of myself

- I am motivated by short-term desires

- I criticise and find fault with everyone

- I have a judgmental attitude

- My happiness does not last

Are you starting to see the pattern?

Can you recognise any of these feelings in yourself?

How do they make you feel?

Now, when I am in soul consciousness: -

- I feel comfortable inside, no matter what happens

- My heart is open and loving

- I love myself

- God becomes my best friend

- My confidence and self-respect soar

- My life has meaning

- I understand the scheme of things

- I attract beauty

- I find what I am looking for

- I become far-sighted

Are you starting to see the contrast?

These two states of being are worlds apart, in fact they are polarities.

In body consciousness: -

- I have low self-esteem and a lot of ego

- I become very defensive

- I have poor listening skills

- I constantly seek approval

- I become possessive and jealous

- I lack integrity

- I can find it hard to let go

- My horizons become limited

- I become affected by the expectations of others

- I hurt those who try to help me

Ouch, can you feel it?

For me, it was like looking in a mirror and, I can tell you, I didn't like what I saw!!

In soul consciousness: -

> - *I understand my story*
>
> - *I see the past, the present and the future clearly*
>
> - *Peace becomes my lifestyle*
>
> - *I become in harmony with the rhythms of nature*
>
> - *Happiness and love fill my mind*
>
> - *I am motivated by wisdom*
>
> - *I understand how the world works*
>
> - *I am not afraid of death or of yesterday*
>
> - *I respect my body and treat it well*
>
> - *My inside matches my outside*

Are you getting the picture?

Do you want a few more?

In body consciousness: -

> - *I have offensive personal habits*
>
> - *I am dependent on physical support systems*
>
> - *I am never satisfied*
>
> - *I become easily bored or lonely*
>
> - *I can be overly sensitive and touchy*
>
> - *I have mood swings*
>
> - *My mind is scattered and cluttered*
>
> - *I leave jobs unfinished, half-way through*
>
> - *I tire easily*

- I say one thing and do another

In soul consciousness: -

- My head and heart move as one

- My highest dreams become reality

- Animals become my friends and I don't eat them

- No human being is my enemy

- I am able to conserve my spiritual and physical energy

- I become a non-violent warrior

- I develop a clear and decisive intellect

- I can easily transform my nature

- Patience and contentment always accompany me

- My body becomes an instrument of positive expression

And on and on we could go.

Maybe you can see just how useful it can be and also how we can change our lives, and so the lives of those around us, just by being soul conscious. These few thoughts, notes and observations have helped me beyond belief. As someone gave these to me, it is my duty and honour to pass them on to you. I think we all want to improve ourselves, even if we won't admit it. If you are able to remain open and detached whilst reading these comparisons, you will notice that the awareness of the body is so natural, that we think that it is normal and that we have to feel this way about ourselves, as if it is our only option.

However, body consciousness is an idea that has become our reality over a period of time, possibly many births, but is not our original state of being. The trick is to practise being soul conscious as much as possible and to make it firm. By doing this, I begin to remember how I used to be. As I practise soul consciousness, I begin to wake-up to who 'I' really am and this awareness becomes my natural nature once again and life becomes easy.

Quite quickly, it has becomes obvious that living my life in soul consciousness is the path to happiness and living life in body consciousness is the route to sadness, low self-esteem, stress and distress. These are conditions that often lead to disease and illness.

The question is, "What do I want?"

"How do I want to feel about myself and the world around me?"

"What is important in my life?"

The more time and energy I put towards being soul conscious, the more clear life becomes. If my mood could be gauged on a thermometer, I would say, the higher the 'mercury of happiness' rises within me. It's so easy; all you have to do is start and watch life change colour before your very eyes!

It's all about beginning or starting a new journey or direction, and this move opens up a whole host of possibilities and opportunities, bringing a sense of joy back into living.

Ego is very slippery. Out of all the negative energies, i.e. anger, desire, attachment, greed and ego, ego is the most invisible. You can see the other negativities, even within yourself, but I am often unable to even know that I have ego. Ego is expressed in arrogance or inferiority. Both, "I am better than..." as well as, "I am no good...," are the two sides of the coin of ego. Whether I am over-confident or have low self-esteem, this is my ego. It puts others down or can undermine the self. If I express this energy, it pushes people away from me and I can become isolated. I can know that I have ego if I have the feeling of being insulted and I experience the pain that goes with it.

In short, I should do myself a favour and 'check and change' myself when it comes to the body conscious attitude of ego. Otherwise, I will fall from a great height at some point as my pride is damaged. Ego only brings sorrow, both for the self as well as others. There is no lasting happiness in ego.

It is time to start to move towards humility, which is a very misunderstood virtue. Humility is not being a doormat and allowing people to walk all over me, but rather it is the dignity and royalty that gives others the chance to express themselves without worry of attack. It's putting others first or offering to help wherever I can. Humility is a strength, not a weakness; it is the foundation of a successfully functioning society.

The Punctured Lung

This incident taught me a few lessons. Firstly, that anything can happen at any time, therefore I should be ever-ready for things to happen suddenly without any prior notice being given.

Secondly, that our past actions (karma) can and will be played out at some point in our lives. This story is about the repercussion of an event that happened in a past life and is explained a little later in another story.

Thirdly, and I think that many people may have experienced this at the time of having an operation; I began to feel very detached from the situation that I was in. This was partly due to the anaesthetic, but also I think that we have some sort of protection mechanism within us that may come into play at a time of trauma.

Funnily enough, I never had any fear, only pain. I thought I was having a heart attack. The only problem was that I was fit, healthy and twenty years old, so it didn't make sense. This particular scene in the drama began whilst I was working in a city wine bar called Grapeshots located in Artillery Passage, London E1. After having studied hotel management at college for a couple of years, I had gained a position as Trainee Manager in a traditional gentleman's luncheon spot in the backstreets of London's financial district. It stood in a narrow alleyway of Whitechapel, made famous by the serial killer 'Jack the Ripper' who used to stalk his victims in the late 1880s.

At work one evening, I was on the phone chatting to my college girlfriend, Lou, just sitting down on a high stool taking things easy around closing time. I felt a small pain followed by a slight change in pressure in the upper chest area on the left hand side and a feeling of a loss of strength. I didn't really take too much notice until the pain sharpened in the collarbone area and the pressure started to cause discomfort. Breathing became laboured and each breath increased the pressure. I could feel my mind beginning to race. "My heart," I was thinking and a barrage of negative thoughts began to enter.

'Winded' was the sensation, and weak. The breath became shallow and reduced. The pain and pressure increased at the edge of the shoulder where it met the collarbone and the pectoral muscle. I was alone in the restaurant and remained cool, but concerned.

As 'last orders' time arrived, which was early, around 8pm as most of the city businessmen had begun their journey home by then, the next challenge would be to close up the wine bar. This involved lifting four, green, solid and very heavy wooden shutters and securing them with iron bars and padlocks. Not much fun in normal circumstances but 'agony' is the word I'd use to describe the task on this particular day as I attempted to lift up each shutter.

Somehow, after pausing for breath many times for each one, I managed to do it. Breathing became more and more difficult. I just couldn't catch my breath and I'd been struggling for over one and a half hours to fill myself with enough oxygen. I staggered to the main city road and an uncomfortable black cab ride of 10 minutes took me to the front door of the company flats in which I stayed, quite near Tower Bridge. Top location, but a bit shabby.

A sharp stabbing pain was travelling across my chest at this point and each breath was shallow and empty. Panic was starting to creep up on me as I gently edged myself out of the cab. I just could not breathe. It was a feeling like drowning, gasping and a battle for each breath. Every second, the pressure increasing. There was an intense pressure in the shoulder. It was as if someone had a rope around my neck restricting the airflow and was crushing my shoulder at the same time! I still had no fear, rather fascination as to what was happening to me.

The stairs up to the first floor flat beat me and I called for help, ringing the doorbell to alert my house mates who raced down to help me. Luckily, Guys (teaching) Hospital was only half a mile from where we lived, but it was still too far to walk in this condition. There was no power left in the body, due to a lack of oxygen over what had been more than 2 hours by now.

We took another taxi and straight into the wheelchair at the hospital. Now, I couldn't walk. Just not enough air and so much pain. I was rushed past a long queue of annoyed looking patients waiting at the A&E

department. I felt so detached from the situation, light-headed and actually, if I'm honest, I was enjoying the excitement and the drama. There was still no fear or any thoughts of dying. I quite liked the idea of the oxygen that was being given to me, thinking that it was surreal and bit like Michael Jackson, who had the habit of carrying oxygen around with him at that time, back in the '80s.

X-rays, checks, tests and one phone call as I was told that I would have to have an operation immediately. I was diagnosed as having a spontaneous pneumothorax, which was caused by a tear in the membrane of the lung, causing it to collapse. As I breathed in, the air spilled out of the lung through the puncture and filled the inside of my ribcage, collapsing the lung across my windpipe.

To the idea of an operation, I immediately thought, "OK, anything to get out of this pain." After a call to my folks, which I think was a bit of a surprise to them, I was taken into the operating room and told that they would have to make another hole in my chest and place a tube into my lung and begin to re-inflate it until the lung was back to normal. The only 'snag' was that they had to keep me awake, conscious, while they were doing the operation.

I was given a local anaesthetic and was asked if I minded a student doctor performing the operation. I agreed, thinking, "Well, he's got to learn somehow." I remember lying on the operating table with my left hand above my head and left side of the body being numb from the 'local', while the student was poking around, between my ribs with a sharp implement, which felt like a corkscrew. Still, I had no actual fear thinking that at least I was in good hands, but anxiety and concern were increasing.

Somehow, there seemed to be a problem, as this kind of corkscrew thing was being jammed between the ribs trying to get between the intercostal muscles and punch another hole in the lung, in order to insert a 1cm diameter tube! Luckily, I hadn't considered what it would feel like to have another hole punched into my lung while I was still awake and watching! It was the chaos and panic that protected me from thinking too much.

He, the student doctor, just couldn't seem to get this corkscrew thing in and I was struggling for breath, now fighting for my life. The atmosphere in the operating theatre had rapidly changed from a learning environment for the new doctor to a full scale 'red alert' as the machines that I was hooked up to started bleeping faster and faster.

Shouts and panicked cries from the nurses as an increasing number of hospital staff arrived in the room. It became 'critical', as I thrashed about, gasping for oxygen and falling into near unconsciousness. I was slipping away, but still I hadn't considered that I would actually die. It was as if I knew, deep down within the programme of the soul, that this was not the end. Although, by now, the situation was very serious. More shouting and chaos, as I began to drift off, probably something to do with the morphine that was being pumped into my veins; I was totally detached from the situation. The senses were no longer working properly. The pain had even gone as my attention was just on breathing. Everything was hazy, but I was still hanging on.

'Shocking' is the only way I can describe what happened next. A surgeon was rushed into the operating theatre and I remember the vibration of the room changing. He knew exactly what to do. His intellect was sharp and he did it with authority, instantly, as soon as he arrived. He stopped the procedure that was taking place in the side of my rib cage, took a cut-throat razor, shaved my chest in the heart area and plunged a metal spike straight through my pectoral muscle, between two ribs and into the membrane of the lung, creating another hole. Don't forget, I was still conscious and awake, just, at this point and watched the whole thing. It was like being blasted with a shotgun at close range. Needless to say, I passed out.

The next week was spent carrying around a tubular column of water about one metre high, with a pipe attached to my chest going into the water valve system. I remember that it gurgled and bubbled whenever I laughed, which was quite amusing to watch. In hindsight, looking back on this experience, I feel that the soul-self knows its part on some level and this is why I felt no fear of death at the time. It was as if I knew that it was not my time to go. Interesting.

Churches

The beginning of my spiritual journey was probably when I was as young as 8 years old. It came in the form of religion and going to church on a Sunday. My mother is a practising Catholic, whose parents originated from southern Ireland in a beautiful little village called Clonakilty, and it's this lineage that first exposed me to God.

Fascinating how we seem to be born into a certain family in order to experience specific things and learn particular lessons that we need to know. You could say that this is also part of our karma or destiny.

As a kid, I was told that I had to go to Church every Sunday. My sister and I would be press-ganged into the car against our wishes and taken to a place of worship. The Catholic Church, St Johns, was the destination of our trip, where we would spend the next hour or so.

My mother, a good lady of strong faith, performed this duty until I was about 14 years old. But I never really understood 'church', probably because at first I was too young and a bit immature and, later, too much of an arrogant teenager. I used to like the idea of God, but just could not get my head around the idea of Jesus being the 'Son of God'. I tried to understand it and even attended Sunday School in one of the buildings of the Church, but it still didn't seem to make any sense to me. I'm sure it was something to do with death.

"What happens when you die," I would ask.

"You go to heaven," I was told.

"Where's that," I asked.

"In the sky," they said, but I already knew about the planets, the sun and the moon, space, galaxies, black holes, supernovas, red dwarfs, the Cosmos, the Universe and the Big Bang.

"So where exactly is heaven then? Which bit is it in?"

I couldn't relate to the Bible either with all its strange old-fashioned words and difficult-to-understand parables. It seemed so out of date. Surely it couldn't be like that, in these modern times of the 1980s, could it?

The church itself had a distinctive smell and, to this day, all of those years of memories get triggered off as soon as I smell a church. The incense, the echo, the height and size, the acoustics are so etched in my mind that I am transported back to those early days as a teenager as soon as I enter one. But you know what? Even though I used to object to going and found it boring, once I was there, I loved the sense of peace and tranquillity. There was such a presence of light; the stained glass windows that were great to look at during the service. Jesus on the cross would always fascinate me; I would become transfixed on his form nailed to the cross.

"I bet that hurt," I thought, but I still didn't get what it was all about. Little did I know that years later I would get first-hand experience of what it feels like to have a stake driven into my body, with the corkscrew thing!

At age 13, I was confirmed. By 14, my mother realised that it was up to me whether I wanted to continue to go to church, even if the relatives didn't approve. So of course, the headstrong 14-year-old didn't bother and would 'hang-out', playing pool at the local sports centre instead.

That was it for Christianity and me. I preferred science. It seemed much more real, up to the minute and exciting, especially space. Now that's what I call 'wicked', man.

The following years took me through a variety of cultures and countries, opening up both my mind and heart to a vast possibility of different lifestyles and ways of living. It was an education of world travel and I was to receive an honorary Master's Degree in studying it practically.

If you've done a bit of backpacking yourself, you'll know what it's like. Grand buildings and cathedrals in Europe; sacred sites and temples in Asia, and Las Vegas in the United States! Not that I was at all interested. Really, I just wanted to get drunk and meet girls and generally have a 'chilled-out' time. But the guide books told me that I should go to these temples, this church, that burial ground, this holy place, oh and don't forget to go the Monkey temple and the holy spring, so I did.

It was like lifetimes of devotion, which I had probably done in the past, being played out in fast-forward, to be experienced but not understood. These travel trips lasted for a few months or even a year at a time. They were sandwiched between intense periods of working, to save money for the next big adventure.

Driven by a thirst for knowledge and a powerful desire to be free, I continued for about 8 years, going and coming, going and coming, saving and spending. Mainly budget travelling, on and on, crossing off different parts of the world map as I went.

Yes, been there. Yes, been there, now where? Looking, but for what? Searching, but not really knowing why. I observed diverse cultures, religions, faiths and civilisations. I was a giant in Timor, Indonesia. Locals were coming up to me and just staring, wanting to touch me, to see if I was real! Back in the early '90s, I don't think they had ever seen anyone like me before, standing 6 foot 2, fair-skinned, hairy and loud. The locals literally couldn't believe their eyes.

'Basic' is the way I would describe the facilities as I stared at the 'Mandi', which was the local word for a shower. However, I would call it a trough of stagnant water, with mosquito larvae floating on it, and a water scoop that looked like a plastic saucepan, which had been chewed by something, maybe a dog or a wolf or a cow or something. This was the ladle to pour the water over your body. No thanks!

I had to get travel out of my system; I just had to know what this planet looked like. Later, my travelling and the journey took a new direction, inwards.

The High Life

Almost everyone has a bit of a wild stage during his or her life; only my wild stage or high life went on a little too long!

At one stage, I was enjoying life as a disc jockey (DJ), playing records in nightclubs and parties. Funny job to have and it is one that creates a false sense of identity even more than most, as the DJ can become a cult hero, leader or way-shower in some social circles. Some use this status symbol title in order to control others and get their own way, however, I just loved music and making people happy.

The music that I played was 'high energy dance music' at 140+ beats per minute and the volume was always loud, and I mean loud. Unnaturally loud, anything up to 40,000 watts. The dance music scene was quite underground in those days of the early '90s - that's another word for small. The people who went to clubs very much looked up to the DJ. It was his job to build the energy and the atmosphere of the club, and take the dancers on a journey to the highest high. The nightclub scene was, as you can imagine, fuelled by alcohol, smoking and a variety of different amphetamines and psychedelics drugs.

How did I fall into this?

Well, it's a long story, but basically, while searching for happiness and not really finding it on my travels, I turned towards an internal search. This journey into the mind and perception took on the form of experimentation with different substances. Always looking for that elusive happiness that I knew existed; I would experiment with different drugs by getting 'high'. This initially came in the form of swallowing a tablet and dancing all night in a seedy south London nightclub. It was dark and hot and sweaty and in the place that played the best music and had the friendliest crowd.

The weekends would be spent 'scoring' various types of recreational drugs and really did make me feel happy, for a while. It was a euphoria that was intoxicating and could be described as 'ecstasy'. 'Rushing' sensations of excitement would be experienced about 45 minutes after taking one of these small tablets. This would be followed by tingling sensations and heavy sweating, increased heart rate and dilated pupils, and a trip to the toilet to empty your bowels or stomach, whichever came first! Disorientation, then mild hallucinations and more rushing with excitement would then continue. Rolling eyeballs, more tingling, more sweating, until, wham, you're 'up'. Up was a word that meant ready, ready to go dancing. Boundless energy, repetitive movement to loud, fast bass-driven music. Mild confusion, speed talking and thinking that everyone was your best mate would then follow. This would last for an hour or two until it was time to take another pill. The next one would be less of a sharp 'come-up' than the first as the senses were now a bit numb and soft, but there would still be an increase of euphoria and an increased high. 'Off Your Face' was the description.

More dancing and talking gibberish and sweating, followed by another pill an hour later. Round and round, popping and dropping, getting gradually higher and higher until the club closed at 6.00am. Then home for smoking marijuana and sex. That was the pattern.

This 'perfect night out' began to wear thin after a while, so a slight change in approach was needed. At this point, which was about 18 months into the phase, the 'comedowns' (i.e. the hangovers) were starting to become a bit grimy and painful. They would last for about 2-3 days afterwards, until the body had rebalanced itself. As we all know, there is always a low after a high. The lows were now starting to outweigh the highs. It was like a mild depression that would last until Wednesday after each weekend. Eventually, it lasted the whole week, until the next weekend. Then more partying! This was a recipe for disaster.

For me, music has always played a big part in my life and from age 9 or 10, when I was given my first transistor radio, I would stay up at night when I was supposed to be sleeping and tune in to pirate radio stations transmitting from the North Sea. Then, after a year or so, I worked out how to record the top-40 pop music show from the radio onto tape cassette, which was kind of illegal, but everyone did it!

The 'Walkman' cassette player was my best friend for years and it would always be threaded onto my belt, with the headphones dangling around my neck or on my head. I always carried spare tapes and batteries 'just in case'. That was way before iPods were even thought about, it must have been around '81. Finally, the CD player was 'invented' in '84 and the quality improved dramatically. I invested in one of the first portable CD player made by Philips in 1987. It would chew up 6 batteries in the time it took for me to travel to work and back, about 1½ hours!

With music, as with most other things in my life, I didn't have much direction; maybe pop and soul to start with, and then the beats started to catch hold of me. First Michael Jackson, Madonna, George Michael, until finally house-music was born. It was a revelation for me.

I began to understand how it worked and which bits of it I liked. This was the true start of my love affair with music. The clubbing gave me an introduction to house music and the next step was to get some 'turntables', some record decks. These record turntables played vinyl records. It seemed like going backwards from CD players, a bit clumsy and bulky, and the chance of scratches and dust reducing the quality. But 'vinyl' was the format that was used by DJs in 1992. The vinyl was much more flexible than CDs as the records could be touched while they were being played on the turntable.

The decks to have were Techniques 1210s and you needed two of them, plus a mixer, with equalisation controls, headphones, amps and speakers, plus, of course, an endless supply of music; I was hooked. Finally, I had found something I liked doing, 'mixing' records. Mixing means, running two vinyl records together at the same speed or beats per minute, which is not easy, that's for sure. I would say it probably took me about 2 years to understand how to do it, as there was no one to teach me and it was quite early days for the DJ scene. I would spend hours each day trying to synchronise two records together, which were pressed at different tempos using small, pitch control levers. I loved 'blending' or 'beat mixing' two tunes together with the mixing desk, varying the 'EQ' to create a third rhythm between the two tracks, 'cross fading', 'dropping' and 'phasing'. I had found a doorway, into another dimension.

As the records blended together, the richness of sound frequency and power would surge through my whole body, sending me into a spin of pleasure, like a comet shooting across the sky of my mind. All my time would be spent mixing records, backwards and forwards, perfecting the style and seamlessness needed to perform live as a DJ to hundreds of people. Taking them on a journey through music, like a shaman or a deity god, during the night of a pumping beat-driven, thunderous, roller-coaster into happiness.

Narcotic-powered, alcohol-enriched, false happiness and 'illusion' inflated the ego to the point of explosion, followed by depression or failure and drug comedowns. I wanted this DJ experience more than anything I had ever come across, not to be the hero playing the records, but for the energy. As the records played out into the nightclub, base pumping, floor vibrating, at ear-splitting volume, the feeling of mixing would send me to a paradise beyond heaven. 'In the mix' was my favourite place to be. This portal, into the unlimited, fascinated me and I craved it.

The reality was that I was addicted to this space and rhythm, between the two records. Weird, I know, but infatuating. I had lost control and began to obsess about this space and the feeling of 'being in the mix'. I would dream about it, have nightmares about failing and even lived out those nightmares in real life. It was such an amazing feeling to be the orchestrator or leader of the crowd of 'ravers'.

As the music pumped through the speakers and was received by those on the dance floor, their energetic response would mirror back towards me, sending shivers down my spine. This energy would increase the excitement, rushing through me, back into the records as I touched them on the decks and shaped them through the mixer. Then expanding, amplified through the speakers, back into the crowd. The spiral of energy continued to increase as the clubbers were sent higher and higher, responding through their hypnotic dance, back into the records and on and on and on to a crescendo of euphoria and carefree pleasure.

I felt like a magician, amazing his audience with dynamics and mystery, anticipation and wonder, like a great conductor leading musicians into and through a symphony. However, the truth was that these fleeting moments of delight were few and far between. The background work, of sourcing, buying and organising the records, finding gigs and parties to play at, the endless practising and networking, became a drag. Not to mention that this lifestyle, of staying up all night, drinking and getting high, was destroying me.

The ego was being both 'fed' and 'starved' at the same time and the result was pain and sorrow, as it always is with ego. I began to lose interest once again and I stopped putting energy and effort into the show. Consequently, I received fewer and fewer bookings, until eventually I had to stop.

After 7 years of focusing everything I had into this avenue, allowing my personal life to slip away from me bit by bit, it was the end. The end of my extrovert stage and time to become introverted. On the way, I had met many strange and beautiful people, many spiritual seekers, and had definitely 'experienced my awakening', but the door to my new life was far from open. I had only begun to turn the key in the lock of consciousness.

In the end, all I was left with was a pair of headphones and the memory. Most of my possessions and my relationships had vanished. The music was the only comfort that remained as my companion.

This rather wobbly period of my beginning left me scared, with anxiety and hopelessness. It was very much the beginning, or preparation, before my serious spiritual efforts could be planted and take root. It made way for a new look at life, as all name and trace of my previous identity had fallen away quite naturally. Although still stuck in old habits, I knew that I deserved more from life than I had ended up with and felt between two worlds, neither here nor there.

I began to read a series of New Age books, ideas and directions, and continued to search for psychics and healers, as well as attending workshops and seminars on a variety of topics. All the time working on myself spiritually, experimenting still with psychedelics, energy and relationships. I had to keep looking.

Fear of failure had restricted my achievements in the past, but now I had nothing more to lose as it had all gone already. I began to understand that the concept of 'mine' is an illusion, for as spiritual beings we own nothing; we are just travellers, on a journey through time, using matter as a support, for a temporary period.

The ego or identity associated with body consciousness had left me broken and weak, hopeless and fearful of more pain. As I began to 'let go', a series of events led me through the 'dark night of the soul' and I began to wake up, gradually realising who I am. I had to fall to the depths of hell, to end up empty and in the gutter for this process to be triggered off.

During this high life period, I had been flying with false happiness, illusion and temporary attainment. Not only had I been travelling away from myself, but also I had been digging a hole big enough to bury my own truth. My awareness was expanding and so was now able to house new ways of thinking and living, but that visit to the 'white witch', which was round about the same time, had sent me spinning into such a new consciousness that it took me a further decade to unravel.

PART 2

THE MIDDLE

The middle is something between a beginning and an end.

It is the time after the development of the beginning and is a stage of expansion and maturity.

The middle of a day is the turning point between the morning and the evening. The middle of a journey is a time in which experience has been gathered. The middle of life is often a time of letting go of the aims and goals of youth, and embracing the present, while preparing for becoming senior. It's a time of maturation and refinement.

This maturity brings new understanding and realisation. It brings a clearer picture of the wholeness of possibilities and potential, whether it's one's own life, one's family or one's plans and ideals.

The awareness of the middle is often the time when we are spurred on to change and adapt to bring about a positive and successful future. As the jigsaw comes together, new methods and approaches are used to achieve our revised, updated and up-graded goals.

The middle is a time of reflection of the beginning and a vision of the desired future.

Newness is a quality that we look for in the middle, something that is fresh and of great worth and importance. In the middle, our values and truth become more important and our morals are crystallised. In the middle, initial infatuation and glitter, of image or of possessions from the beginning period, become less influential. This maturity brings us our greatness.

The middle section of this book is expressed through stories that invite you to examine your development and growth. It presents alternatives in living and thinking.

The Lost Diamond

This is a nice story that was created by a group of teachers to help to present Raja Yoga Meditation. It's very simple, yet can somehow open our minds to new possibilities, and give us understanding as to why things are the way they are.

It almost feels like a fairy tale, but hey, life is a bit of a fairy tale isn't it; sometimes good and sometimes wicked.

Once upon a time, there was a prince who was given a beautiful diamond by his father, the king, which he valued highly as his most precious possession. Simply possessing the diamond made him feel peaceful, loving and happy. However, one day he lost hold of the diamond, which dropped and rolled into a pond and sank to the bottom. He searched and searched for the diamond, but it was nowhere to be seen. After a long search and feeling sad, knowing that he had lost something very precious, he continued on with his life, always sensing that something was missing.

Over the autumn and winter, debris gathered on the pond, twigs and dead leaves mixed with the accumulated rubbish. The pond became stagnant and a thick layer of algae covered the surface. Anyone coming across the pond would never imagine that deep down below was the most beautiful and precious diamond, for they would only see the top of the pond, the algae and dead leaves.

This is our story.

We are the diamond, the 'spiritual diamond', with beautiful qualities of purity, peace, love, wisdom and joy. However, over time, we forgot and lost sight of who we were, the diamond, and started to forget our true qualities. Instead, using only our physical eyes, we identified with just the body and the accumulated mixture of positive and negative experiences that has affected us over time.

Imagine what would happen if the bus driver thought that he was the bus!

This is exactly what we do when we think that we are the body and this is why we have become confused in the world today. Everything is upside down and back to front. We begin to believe that the body is who we are and the negative experiences are all part of living life.

Once we begin to practise being soul conscious and as this becomes our self-belief, negative traits have less impact on us. The 'algae' is anger, greed, desire, attachment and ego, and to become free from this negativity, we just need to focus on our true positive nature.

For when you focus on consciousness, it expands.

What does this mean?

Well, whatever I think about will get bigger inside my mind and expand. So the question is, "What do I want?" Because, whatever I begin to think about will get bigger and will eventually become my experience within the world.

Quite a responsibility, huh?

The Power of Collective Meditation

When meditation takes place in any given area, especially if it is in a group, the vibration of the energy within that locality rises. By 'vibration', I mean the spiritual quality of the atmosphere.

Often, when meditation is practised in an area that is known for violence, the crime rate actually goes down, its impact is that strong. The power of the mind is such that, when it is harnessed in a positive way, it can bring about great changes, not only in the self, but also in the environment.

You could say that the most powerful energy on this planet is not nuclear weapons or even Nature, but is the human mind. Nature itself is influenced by our minds.

When we are disrespectful to the Earth, greedy and irresponsible, she reacts accordingly. Therefore, if we can create positive thoughts and thinking patterns, and take action accordingly, Nature will respond positively. This is what is beginning to happen as we take charge of our actions and start to recycle, reuse and reduce our consumption of resources.

The question is, "Have we left it a little late to begin to undo the negative thought patterns of our irresponsible past?"

I've heard it said that meditation is so powerful that, when practised in the correct way, it can 'change the direction of the atom'.

What does this mean?

Well, for me it means transforming the negative into positive.

Water molecules, which actually have a memory storage space within them, can be transformed into perfect crystal formations by sending positive, powerful thoughts towards them. In the same way, negative thoughts also impact the water, distorting and disrupting the crystal structure. Don't forget, our bodies are over 70% water, so sending positive thoughts towards others and ourselves can create health, rather than illness.

We need to become responsible for our thoughts. They are powerful devices of 'mass creation'.

On a personal level, a relationship can be healed, or even transformed, through sending positive thoughts to another person. This is something I practised at the time I was separating from my wife. If you have been through that experience yourself, you will know how painful it is and how all communication can easily break down due to high emotion, frustration, guilt and misunderstanding.

During my meditation, I would visualise filling myself with light, peace and love, and then send positive energy to my ex-wife; seeing us interacting together in a calm and pleasant way. After regular practice of this meditation, our relationship is now better than ever, which is more than I could ever have hoped. It was well worth the effort. The resentment and pain were cleared, and there is a level of regard and respect that did not exist while we were together.

Positive thinking and meditation have also given me enthusiasm for life and made even the mundane activities, that we still have to perform, easy and pleasurable.

Life is no longer 'pointless' and I am able to see benefit in everything. The word 'boring' no longer exists in my awareness and has been replaced with 'being'.

Radio Signal Receiver

Healing myself and my relationships, as well as healing the global environmental vibration, is not a small task. It is not something that I can do alone. Yes, reconnecting to myself as a soul or spiritual being is the first step, but I also need to connect to the Source. It's only when I become an instrument who can be used by God that things can really change.

Connecting to the Supreme Soul, the Divine Energy that is always giving through meditation, is a bit like tuning-in to a radio station with an old-fashioned radio set. To start, you have to turn the dial to the right place on the receiver to hear the signal clearly. If you turn it too much, it becomes out of tune and distorted. If you don't turn it enough, it remains crackly. If you get it just right, the signal is received loud and clear and you are tuned into the music or rhythm of life.

A Radio Station, like the Supreme Energy, is always transmitting out to everyone all the time, but you can only hear it, or Him, if you tune in accurately. Meditation is the same. If you tune into the Divine, you will find that He is constantly giving positivity and is 'unlimited' in that giving. The only question then is, "How much do I want to take?"

These days, it's all digital radios and one-touch tuning. Soul consciousness is like digital tuning on the radio. As soon as we switch to soul consciousness, we can automatically connect to the Supreme loud and clear, and can receive light and unconditional love from Him immediately. 'Soul consciousness is one-touch tuning'.

The Two Wolves

It's when we have experience that has been gained from our beginning, that teaching and facilitation can be shared in the middle. Understanding can then be experienced with maturity and we are more able to be of service to others. The following little story I heard many years ago illustrates this concept very nicely.

An old Cherokee Indian is teaching his grandson about life.

"A fight is going on inside me," he said to his grandson. "It is a terrible fight between two wolves." "One is evil. He is anger, envy, sorrow, regret, greed, arrogance, self-pity, guilt, resentment, lies, false pride, superiority and ego. The other is good. He is joy, peace and love, hope, serenity, humility, kindness, benevolence, empathy, generosity, truth, compassion and faith. This same fight is going on inside you and every other person too."

The grandson thought about this for a minute and then asked his grandfather, "Which wolf will win?"

The old Cherokee replied, "The one you feed."

Billy Graham

Happiness

The original quality of the soul is happiness.

Due to past situations and experiences we have been through in life, our happiness has diminished and so we start to look for it outside of ourselves.

The external happiness that we look for outside ourselves is temporary and is subject to limitation. It can be taken away at any moment, plunging us into sadness, emptiness and depression. Realising that I am a being of happiness and diving deep into the self-soul in silence, I can relocate my own stock of happiness and begin to replenish it, by connecting to the 'Supreme Source' of happiness. This connection is like plugging into the 'mains supply' and downloading unlimited amounts of happiness.

The question then is, "How much happiness can I take?"

This type of happiness does not depend on any situation, environment or person, so avoids the roller-coaster of highs and lows, which we associate with wanting, receiving and losing. With true happiness there is a sense of stability and balance. Life becomes even. This is a good foundation on which to build relationships and our life in general.

In the face of adversity, souls like Nelson Mandela are able to maintain their 'stock' of happiness and donate it to others, even if those others are causing difficulties. There are many others who have mastered this skill and so become abundant with happiness, shining light in the darkness. They are the diamonds, amplifying the light and radiating, from every facet, multi-coloured rays of all virtues and qualities of the human soul. This then becomes their nature. It is so attractive, so magnetic and so charismatic.

Observe such people when you find them. They are sparkling with light from their eyes and forehead, a true pleasure to be around them and in their presence, even if only for a few seconds.

The Key to Happiness

Here's another little gem I loved when I heard it, originating from a Hindu legend. Author unknown.

Imagine a time when the gods were creating the Earth. They created the seas and the oceans; they created the forests and the whole of nature. They created the planets, the stars, and the sun and the moon. The stage was set for the drama of life to begin. They sat back and were pleased with their work. They then decided to put the actors onto the stage. First they put all the animals and living creatures. Then they put the first man and woman. They had finished.

But the head of the gods said, "Wait, we have forgotten one thing." In his hand, he had the 'Key to Happiness'. All the gods started arguing about where to put the key. "Let's put it on the moon," said one, "It will never be found there." "Let's put it at the deepest point of the ocean," said another, "They will never find it there."

"No," said the head of the gods. "They will find it in those places. But if we put the key inside their own hearts, they will never think of looking there! Then we can all amuse ourselves watching them go to the moon and go to the bottom of the ocean looking for it."

Where is it that we are looking for our own happiness? This is a very revealing question to ask ourselves. For this question, we will need a great deal of humility, honesty and courage, in order to be able to accept the answer that we receive

The Benefits of being Bodiless

Our eternal nature is that of being bodiless, but it's just that we have forgotten.

As spirits, we come bodiless into our 'chosen' body. This is determined by our previous actions. We leave bodiless, as souls, leaving an old costume behind and move towards a new experience in this physical world, once again as a result of our actions.

When we identify with being a body too much, it then becomes our 'normal nature' and this is how we become limited in our awareness and spiritual power. The problems come when we exist only in this body conscious state without exploring the dimension of the soul-self. In turn, this narrow viewpoint can cause sorrow and a sense of loss when we feel that, if we are the body, we can die and so lose our life.

This 'fear of dying' or loss of the body is the root cause of all fear. It is created and sustained by our lack of awareness of truth or understanding that 'I', as a soul, am eternal. I am always bodiless anyway and am just in this body for a short period of time in order to know and experience myself. Therefore, the question then becomes, "Bodiless, why not?" Rather than, why?

Here's an experience I had that helped me to grasp this concept in a very obvious way. It happened during a trip to India. Whilst practising meditation in quite a large group, I experienced a switch of awareness take place within me.

The meditation was of a 'guided' variety, whereby one person leads the group into a visualisation through speaking a commentary highlighting the qualities of the soul and takes the practitioners into feelings and then experience. It was deep and mind-expanding, so much so that the words triggered feelings, and even sensations and memories, which allowed me to become extremely detached from the awareness of the body.

The body was still, comfortable and safe on the chair, but with my mind and intellect, I was flying on the power of thought and quite oblivious of the body. I was concentrated and enjoying playing internally with these visualisations, creating a picture, feelings and emotions of being above and beyond the physical world.

As all traces of stress and tension melted away, there was a free flow of emotions and the relief of letting go. I became joyful, liberated and felt completely beyond limits.

In this timeless space, I was unaware of my body, the surroundings, others around me, where I was and how I got there, or even for how long I had been there. It just didn't matter. Everything was fine and wonderful, and I was truly above the body and of having to look after it, for a while anyway. I was still connected with the body, but my conscious awareness was of soul. It was a glimpse of the truth.

Detached and full of love and light, I became aware of movement around me. Everything was soft and subtle, and there was no sharpness to sounds or images, just like when you wake up gently in a comfy place. As the activity intensified a little and I started to have more of a sense of the scene that I was sitting in, it was as though I had just 'landed' or incarnated into this body, in the temple of the forehead, after having been on a journey.

I waited and watched the people leaving the hall peacefully, enjoying the show and this feeling of light and lightness. It was as if energy was 'pulsing' down through my body and I gradually was able to feel the shoulders, the arms resting on the legs, but strangely still not feeling the legs.

Slowly everything became reconnected and I was back, back fully connected to and with my body, charged with power and full of light. I felt a softness and easiness and looseness of the body, as if it were just baggy clothes.

By this time, the hall was nearly empty. I sat almost alone, but not lonely, as I had just experienced a 'link of love' and compassion with the Supreme Being. I was full and overwhelmed with contentment. I wiped away the tracks of my tears, released through the emotional patch of the journey, and began to stand slowly. Another person passed by and shot me a look that said to me that she knew exactly what I had just been through. Maybe it was still showing on my face and in my vibration. She checked whether I was OK to stand and I gestured yes, but slowly. Still no need to come into sound and speak. That seemed just too 'gross' and raw at this stage.

Dinner was next, as it was that time in the evening, but 'dinner' had no concept for me. Food? Not really. It seemed too solid. Such a strange idea to feed the body, for there was no hunger. Everything was just 'smooth' and so no need to change anything right now.

Walking the 300 metres from the hall to the dining room was bliss. Walking, no, floating, and not quite touching the ground. I was 'super sensitive' with a heightened state of awareness. Gliding, light as air, beaming with joy. Noticing things that I had never seen before, colour, radiance and life. Energy flows overlaid and tinted everything. I could 'see' beings inside their bodies; each soul (being) was using the machinery of its body, depending on its consciousness, according to its awareness. I could see that some beings had tremendous understanding that they were souls and so effortlessly guiding their vehicle (body) regardless of the age or health of that body. They had a 'fluid' relationship between mind, body and soul. Other beings with less understanding seemed clumsy and awkward, jerky and stiff with body consciousness even if their body was much younger and fitter.

I wondered, "Why did they not tell me about this earlier? Why had they kept it to themselves and not shared this with me?" Everything seemed so obvious now, so easy, simple and pure. Natural.

How come I hadn't noticed this before? How had I missed it? "Of course," I realised, "each one is moving along with a different depth of understanding. It's just that now, I too can 'see' what they can see all the time." I had the same perception, and vision as them, temporarily, due to the earlier meditation I had been practising.

I did take some food and it did seem weird. I was just playing along with the 'game', the scene that I found myself in at that time; the Dinner Scene. I played my 'part' and everything tasted different.

The feeling of being royal, like a prince, stayed with me all evening until I went to bed. Then when I awoke in the morning, once again, I was back to normal. Shame. I liked that soul conscious feeling and I vowed to find it again. After all, practice makes perfect. Everyone has his or her perfect form and that is a good aim to have - the aim to reach our own, perfect stage.

Altered States

I was always interested in altered states. I liked having all sorts of different experiences. At one point, I even enjoyed getting the flu or a cold or being ill, just so I could observe what was happening in my body that was different and take some medicine to see what that did. It would always be a kind of an experiment. Strange, I know, but true.

I liked 'different', something other than normal. Normal was just too limited, insignificant and basic. It was too ordinary. I liked rocket-powered or sky dive, roller coaster types of feelings, not normal. The more cosmic the experience, the better, hence the experimentation with psychedelic drugs, such as LSD and magic mushrooms, at one stage on my journey.

This expansion of my awareness and the otherworldly dimensional experiences were both exciting and fascinating. The only concern really, apart from the cost, was of how much to take and in what time period to achieve maximum effect, making sure not to 'overdo' it of course at the same time. And anyway, how do you know how much is too much or if it just wouldn't quite be enough, which it never seemed to be?

It was a constant battle and regular pastime over a quite 'wobbly' phase in my mid to late twenties. Some of the experiments were quite 'ground-breaking' in their impact, but, at the end of the day, there is no real or tangible benefit to the soul with this self-destructive behaviour. In fact, yes, there were momentary glimpses of other dimensions, which are not normally perceived in everyday life, but at the cost of a lack of clarity and a complete inability to remember what had actually happened anyway. It's like finding the answer to the Universe and then forgetting where you put it when you fell asleep.

There were a couple of outstanding episodes however, which sent my consciousness beyond the parameters that we call normal. One of these journeys, took me through a sky of floating golden orbs and into a dark formless place where liquid was breathed as air and an uneasy 'hissing' sound became quite disturbing to the non-specific, non-physical, non-locatable observer, me.

Another shaman-style 'trip' into other realms gave the experience of reality and, in fact, all physical forms folding up like paper templates into two-dimensional 'flatness' without any depth! Apart from being able to actually look between the planes of reality, between the very layers of physical existence, this didn't help me at all in my understanding of who I am and why I am here. In fact, 'pointless and scary' can describe it for me, although I did like the visuals that sometimes occurred, such as whirlwinds, vortex-type energy spins and a reconstruction of matter into the image of sitting on a chunk of earth the size of a football field, gently floating through space. Nice.

The magic mushroom gave the most secrets away. Such an innocent little fungi really was a 'fun guy'. He was subtle, but strong. He was delicate, yet disruptive. He was minute, yet mighty. Growing in the mud, yet able to unlock the 'blueprint' of each and every blade of grass with a glance. I heard that they (magic mushrooms) arrived on the Earth on the back of meteors flying through space in order to spread consciousness. Good story, but I doubt it.

The explosion of visual colour and sensitivity was the attraction. As I ingested them, the psilocybin metabolised, sending firework-like explosions of internal euphoria and joy through the body, hand in hand with rushes of love, happiness and light. It all seemed like a fairy tale delight until, yes, I just did one too many of the small apple-sized Mexican variety and paid a huge price.

'Poison' is the only way I can describe it, moving from pleasure into extreme physical pain and absolute terror and fear. I think it is the most scared I have ever been in all my life and I have been in some pretty tricky situations in this lifetime, I can say. That was it; it put me right off. I just stick to the ones you can buy in the supermarket now, and they taste really good sautéed in olive oil.

Ecstasy. This is the one that damaged me the most I think, both mentally and psychologically as well as spiritually. I loved it. That was the problem and, initially, it loved me and then it didn't. At the beginning, it was a light and fluffy 'loved-up' experience, as everyone seemed to be your best friend, but, after time, it turns 'dark and moody' as well as bitter, twisted and self-destructive.

'E' was very much connected to sex for me and, at one point I was unable to separate the two. It was such a degraded drive and desire, and could only lead to sorrow. This journey spanned nearly a decade. Addicted, well physically not, but psychologically definitely hooked. So there it is, the 'narcotic phase'. I'm not proud of it, but I did approach it in a very 'scientific' way. Each encounter was a new 'experiment' into consciousness and perception, trying to find truth, seeing just how far I could go. In many ways, having to give it a try, just in case the answers were there. But of course, they weren't.

It is a very slippery slope and definitely not one that I would endorse. It only brings ill health, pain and sorrow. Do I regret it? "Well, no,… it was just part of the game!" Do I recommend it? "Definitely not!" You just can't win with those things; it's just another ball and chain around your leg.

The one that I haven't mentioned so far is 'puff' or weed, hash, dope, spliff, solids, ganja, gear, whatever you want to call it. It's all marijuana. I did like to enjoy smoking it, and often. 'Scoring' (this means getting supplied), I would search for it in every part of the world that I travelled. It's never hard to find and was always a good adventure. Many amusing stories were enacted and unfolded in the process of scoring. It was a very 'accepted' substance, often considered as a medicine in many places, with varying quality and different purity. I studied this natural remedy in a very practical manner. It was such a beautifully peaceful pastime. I enjoyed a 'smoke', whether on the beaches of Thailand, in the mountains of Nepal, in the forest festivals of Portugal or in urban London Town. It was always non-violent and reflective for the soul.

It wasn't the tobacco that I liked, but it was a 'joint' (hand-rolled cigarette of tobacco mixed with marijuana). Like a perfect masculine/feminine balance of the natural rhythm of nature Herself.

From morning till night, I engaged myself in rolling up a 'spliff' and 'puffing'. I claimed the title 'Stoner', meaning that I was always 'stoned' (high on marijuana smoke) and this gentle, peaceful, detachment from the world was very much how you could describe my nature.

Rolling, smoking, chilling and running out of gear, then scoring some more, this was the lifestyle that I indulged in for years. This routine underpinned everything. It also led to an absolute lack of self-respect. I just couldn't give a 'damn' about anything. Peace is what I wanted and a cough is what I got, as well as the 'munchies'. This is when you have a craving for sweets, snacks or convenience food, and it is uncontrollable, unnatural and unavoidable!

It wasn't that I was a bad guy; I was just lost and unable to find the path. I was in a trap and stuck, making the same mistakes over and over again. Unhappy, unlucky and unswerving in my approach to life. I was heading in completely the wrong direction and out of control.

If my body were the bus, it would have been written off. This driver (soul) was driving with 'undue care and attention'. It would be like driving at full speed up the motorway, but in the wrong direction! It would be like reversing down a mountain road! Or simply filling the bus with the wrong type of fuel and expecting it to go where and when you want it to!

'Change', that's what was needed. I needed a change in attitude and awareness towards my journey. It would need to be holistic, not just a quick fix, short-term change, but an overhaul. This bus (my body) would need to be taken off the road (out of this lifestyle) and rebuilt from the inside (soul) outwards. Quality parts (spiritual knowledge) would need to be used, with patience, love and care (virtues), and bit-by-bit the rebuild (transformation) would be complete.

All I needed to do was start, "But how? "

So I read all sorts of books, trying to find the elusive 'instruction manual' for a better life, and the 'road map' of where to go and how to get there.

The Bigger Picture

Being able to see with a broad vision or through a wide-angle lens can help us to accept situations and circumstances as they are, without becoming upset or wanting to change them. This encourages tolerance and nourishes compassion, which then inspires co-operation.

The 'bigger picture' includes all events and possibilities. It shows us that it is only when we are able to observe an entire system that we can fully understand its value and purpose. It takes a certain level of maturity to understand the past, the present and the future, and it's often during the middle (adulthood) of our journey that we can reach this stage of awareness.

A system may be mechanical, as with the bus, it may be biological, like the body, or even environmental, as in the world in which we live. It's when we can stand back from a system and see the whole picture that things begin to come into focus and make sense.

The River Thames, which flows through London UK, is a good example.

If you were to take a snapshot photo of the Thames River as it passed through the centre of London, you would see a wide, dirty river, full of mud and silt, plastic bags and even supermarket shopping trolleys and old tyres. If you showed this picture to someone in say, Australia, he would say, "G'day mate, your river's a bit dirty, I wouldn't like to take a dip in that, cobber" or something like that. He would think that the whole river is like that; according to the photo snapshot you gave him to look at.

However, he doesn't know that the River Thames starts in a Gloucestershire field near Cirencester, about 175 miles away from where the picture that you showed him had been taken. At its start, it is a spring, supplied by water from deep beneath the earth.

Then, as it runs through the valleys of Gloucestershire, it forms a stream that joins other streams, gradually getting bigger with fresh clean, clear water running through the countryside of Oxfordshire.

At this stage, the River Thames is crystal clear, with plenty of fish swimming in it and wildlife enjoying its course. Birds and animals use it as their habitat and it is lined with trees and bushes for miles and miles. It's a nice picnic spot for many during the summer months and plenty of people swim in it when the weather's warm enough.

Our imaginary Australian wouldn't see that as it gets bigger, it slows down and widens, until eventually passing through the centre of London, which is where he will finally recognise it from the picture that we gave him. After that, it continues to widen and passes through the industrial area of east London, probably gets filled with chemicals and waste, before it runs out past Tilbury and into the North Sea.

In time, the sun will cause some of the water in the sea to evaporate, rising up into the sky to form clouds. The wind will blow those clouds across to Gloucestershire where they will empty the water vapour as rain, which will fall onto the fields and replenish the water deep beneath the earth so that it can spring again as the source of the Thames River.

This is the Bigger Picture.

The snapshot is misleading, to say the least, as it only shows part of the river system.

The state of our consciousness now is also only a snapshot. The bigger picture is that once, like the Thames, our consciousness was pure, clean, alive, fast-flowing and vibrant. The state of our consciousness now is not the least help in being able to understand where we once were, or where we are going.

The bigger picture also applies to our relationships.

I know that I was distraught and devastated at the time I went through the divorce from my wife. I could only see that moment, i.e. the snapshot of that event. I did not realise at the time that that was exactly what I had to go through in order to be where I am now, i.e. happy and content. This is the bigger picture.

So you could even say that, in viewing the bigger picture, there is benefit in everything.

Look at the seasons. During the winter everything looks dead and, if you were a Martian landing on the Earth that day, you would think that it is always like that on Earth. Only when the spring begins, and the trees and plants start to grow again, would our Martian friend say, "Maybe it's OK here after all."

This is seeing the bigger picture.

Our True Value

It's around about the middle of something that we begin to see its true value. It's at this time that enough experience and information has been gained to come to that type of conclusion.

We are incredibly valuable and very precious living-lights. We are spiritual beings made in the image of the Supreme Soul. As She is a point of living light, so we are points of living light/energy. We are all children of the Divine Parent.

I find I have to remind myself of this many times each day, and find it uplifting and beautiful to reflect on this during moments of meditation.

This little story can help us grasp the concept of value and to see how our mind can play tricks on us if we are careless with our thoughts or become influenced by the judgments of others and of society.

A speaker was giving a talk at a conference.

He pulled out a new crisp 50-pound note from his pocket and held it up and asked the audience, "Who would like this note?"

Most people put their hand up.

He then threw it on the ground and stepped on it and asked the audience the same question.

This time less people put up their hands. He then picked up the note and spat on it and again asked the audience the same question.

This time, very few people raised their hands.

He then said, "The value of the 50 pound note remains the same, whether it is crisp and new or filthy and dirty."

He continued, "In the same way, no matter what life experiences we go through, we may be pushed around, misused and trodden on, but our value remains the same."

Author Unknown

Would you agree?

Yoga

The word 'yoga' means union or connection.

This firstly refers to the connection or union of the self-soul through understanding, knowledge and reflection of its own qualities, virtues and specialties. Knowing the self-soul as a being of light, eternal and unique.

There are many different types of yoga, whether postures or 'pranayama' (breathing exercises). There are a variety of different styles of teaching that go with them.

There is also Raja Yoga Meditation, which expands the understanding of the self and the world around us by connecting to the Source, the Supreme Soul, the Knowledge-full One. It's this aspect which has most interest to me and has fascinated me for more than a decade.

In the past, I very much enjoyed practising Iyengar and Ashtanga Yoga, as well as Kundalini Yoga, which are all a series of 'asana' or positions. These types of yoga tone and strengthen not only the muscles, tendons and bones of the body, but also the internal organs which become 'maintained' through these positions. The mind is also used in a positive way, focusing on balance, grace and using the power of determination to complete these sometimes exhausting, but always rejuvenating, workouts.

The energetic fields of the body or 'chakras' are also realigned through these forms of yoga and there is a general feeling of wellbeing and vitality that I have not experienced from any other activity. I have always been a regular swimmer and enjoyed many team games as a youngster, but yoga was a step into the spiritual, mind, body and soul relationship.

I found many minor physical health issues were resolved through yoga, without any specific focus on them. In a nutshell, yoga is good for you. However, there is still limitation. There is limitation of ability, time and space, flexibility and gravity, etc. These are all the normal limitations of the physical world that we have become accustomed to.

Meditation is different.

Meditation is a 'vehicle' for moving into the unlimited and beyond the feeling of the temporary, small world that we live in. With regular practice, it is possible to experience other dimensions of existence, by using the mind and intellect, which are inside me, the soul. I am the non-physical being of light within this body. The mind and intellect are not me, but are my co-operative helpers in experiencing myself in my highest form.

During meditation, one can become free from the effect of lower energies such as anger, lust/desire, greed, ego, attachment and even beyond fear. Being truly fearless and able to fly on wings of zeal and enthusiasm and courage, so to speak. Being in the zone, the soul-conscious zone. In this zone, there is the experience of freedom, liberation and 'want-less-ness'.

I find that I am constantly trying to maintain a balance of equilibrium when I am in the consciousness of being a body. Either I want food, water, coffee, excitement, the toilet or something or another. There is no chance of stillness in body consciousness. However, when in the zone, I am content. Everything is fine just as it is. No need to keep constantly checking the body, dealing with a massive amount of data and information that is entering though the eyes, ears or other sense organs. This data then has to be processed through the brain and resolved through actions. This process is constantly going on from morning till night!

Exhausting or what!?

In the zone of soul consciousness, there is peace, stillness and calm. This sense of peace is atmospheric and the nearby vicinity becomes charged with the vibration of peace in the form of lightness. Not physical light, although that is also there sometimes, but a feeling as though the density of everything has been reduced and become lighter, less heavy or more subtle. A feeling of lightness in relationship to the body increases and a distinct awareness of separation or disassociation begins to seep into the consciousness. This is my actual experience of being bodiless. It's a most beautiful experience. It feels safe and secure. The feeling is like being still connected or in connection with the body, but yet next to it at the same time. I feel unaffected or pulled by any desire or need of the body, both loving to it and detached from it.

Like a beautifully coloured bird, flying out of a golden cage that is far too small for it and flapping its wings. Once again, free to fly and always able to return to the cage if it needs to for any reason. It's a feeling of space with unlimited aliveness. But let's face it, which bird would want to be stuck in a cage, even if it is golden, once they have experienced the sky?

At the beginning, when I first felt this bodiless, out-of-body feeling, I was elated, ecstatic with joy and wanted to maintain the feeling for ever. And trust me, this bit is just the start, it gets better, much better. This feeling is just the bonus, not the aim or goal. That comes later. Although this is just my personal experience, everyone is different. For me, it's a feeling of being timeless, bodiless, genderless, ageless, and just not 'pulled' by limitations and confines. It's like being 'beyond' and subtle.

Once I have reconnected to myself and my original qualities, my attention returns to my 'Home of Light'. You could say a kind of soul world, which is the original residence of all souls before they come to this physical world to play. It is also the place where we all return once the 'play' is over. In this unlimited world of golden-red bliss, there is only stillness and silence, no movement, no form, just rest; true rest, nowhere to go, nothing to do, just to be. It's also the home of the Supreme Soul and it's this Divine Being that I connect to in a link, a union of love during Raja Yoga Meditation. Here I recharge with His unending rays of all positive energies. I feel as though I am recharging the battery of the soul by plugging into the mains supply of all positive energy, the Supreme.

It feels wonderful, like floating in an ocean of unconditional love on the waves of happiness and wisdom, in a sea of peace and power, at rest with the one Father. Perfect.

This is the aim.

All the other stuff is extra, a bonus and the ride to get to this point of stillness. No thoughts here, no desire or want, just acceptance. Nice. This really is a place I don't want to come back from, because nothing can 'top' this experience. It is the 'apex', the highest of heights and the 'daddy' of all feelings.

Maintaining this awareness and sustaining it has been my goal in life ever since my first encounter. I now know that I do have to come back down here into the physical world, not only to drive the bus, but also to tell all my brothers and sisters that it's there. To tell them, that there is more to life than the stress of survival and the chaos of an uncertain and unstable future. A lot more.

My role now is to help others to experience themselves as souls, beings of light, and reach their Home of Light, with the power of the mind and intellect, through Raja Yoga.

Breaking Habits

Solving problems and finding solutions is a very positive way of living. I may need to reform my activities and refine my ideals in order for this to take place.

Habits are patterns that can often hold us back from reaching our potential and it's these habits that we need to break in order to free ourselves from our own self-imposed limitations.

Smoking was one of my habits and I smoked for over 10 years. I tried to stop many times, but could only last a few days before a situation would make me turn to the habit once again! I had handed all my power over to those nicotine sticks! I realised that the only way I could break the habit for good was to replace it with something that was more powerful, positive and constructive. My problem was that I was addicted to the feeling of calm and peace, and the only way I thought I could get that was to smoke 'joints' of marijuana.

As I started to practise meditation, I began to experience a similar feeling of peace and silence, but with this there was clarity and a deep understanding of truth. The 'dope' just made me lazy and forgetful; the meditation gave me hope and freedom to fly with the power of positive thoughts. The dope made me into a slobbering moron, unable to even communicate with anyone or anything. The meditation made me rich in all spiritual powers and qualities, as well as virtues and specialities. The dope made me poor from trying to satisfy my habit. The meditation began to build a positive outlook on life and the world, and my part within that.

The marijuana trapped me into anti-social behaviour and mental addiction. The meditation saved me from myself, or rather from my desires and negative thought patterns.

So the two activities, which look on the surface to give the same feeling of peace, were actually opposites. One was a downward spiral to self-pity and the other the road to freedom, true peace and enlightenment. Enlightenment to me is 'knowing', knowing who I am and knowing to whom I belong. I am a soul and I belong to the Supreme Parent, the Ocean of Love, Peace and Happiness, the Divine, God, the Father, the Teacher and the Guide. This became my silent mantra.

Any bad habits can be transformed with the power of Raja Yoga Meditation. The very realisation or understanding of the self and God are able to transform any negativity into positivity.

Each soul is originally good and, due to its past experiences and situations, has fallen to its present state. With this understanding, I cannot judge a soul, as each one is playing its role perfectly and according to its 'script', but I can judge its actions for rightness or wrongness. After all, how do we know what each soul has been through to make it the way that it is now?

By separating the being from its actions, I am able to remain as a detached observer and witness or observe each scene of the drama. Once I can maintain this position, I can become free from the influence of situations or people. Then through meditation, I can firstly rebalance myself, overflow positive energy like a fountain and shower all beings with light, helping them to transform themselves and return to their original state of positivity.

Easy…

Letting Go

This is another story that encourages us to see our habit of holding on to the pressures of life. Letting go is the trick to experience life as a joy, as a dance.

A professor began his class by holding up a glass with some water in it. He held it up for all to see and asked the students, "How much do you think this glass weighs?"

"50 grams, 100 grams, 125 grams." The students answered.

"I really don't know unless I weigh it," said the professor, "But my question is, what would happen if I held it up like this for a few minutes?"

"Nothing," the students said.

"OK, what would happen if I held it up, like this for an hour," the professor asked?

"Your arm would begin to ache," said one of the students.

"You are right. Now what would happen if I held it up for a day?"

"Your arm would go numb, you might have severe muscle stress, paralysis, have to go to hospital for sure," ventured another student and all the students laughed.

"Very good, but during this, did the weight of the glass change?" asked the professor.

"No," the students said.

"Then what caused my arm to ache and the muscle to stress?"

The students were puzzled. "You kept holding on to the glass," said one of the students.

"Exactly," said the professor.

"Life's problems are sometimes like this. Hold them for a few minutes in your head and they seem OK. Think of them for a long time and they begin to ache. Hold them even longer and they begin to paralyse you," he continued.

Then he went on, "You will not be able to do anything. It is important to think of challenges (problems) in your life, but even more important to put them down at the end of every day before you go to sleep. That way you are not stressed. You wake up every day fresh and strong and can handle any issue or challenge that comes your way."

The professor smiled and concluded, "Remember to put the glass down today."

Author Unknown

If we become paralysed by something that has happened in the past, then that person or situation stills 'owns' us. We are still held 'hostage' by that event and it affects our present moment, not allowing us to experience the fullness of NOW.

When I let go, I become light and this lightness is attractive; it attracts new and fresh experiences and gives me a sense of freedom. I can then become carefree, not careless, and enjoy the richness of what life has to offer, rather than being distracted by an old broken record, going round and round in my mind.

So letting go is connected to fearlessness. Can you imagine how it would be to live without fear?

Often, young children are carefree and fearless. This is because they are not holding on to past experiences which may have caused them to become scared. It is not that we should have no regard for danger, but that we don't see everything as 'dangerous'.

When we can let go of the things that are out of our control and learn from past experience, our minds and intellects are free to create an enjoyable present and a rich and rewarding future. Then we can put a full stop to any negative experiences of the past and get on with living life to the fullest.

Don't give sorrow and definitely don't accept sorrow from others.

We do have a choice. So, what do you choose to accept?

Just give 'good wishes', to all and that is what will come back to you.

It's the Universal law of Cause and Effect (Karma).

The Glass of Dirty Water

Let's take a very simple example of a glass filled with dirty water and then we ask the question, "How is it possible to have the same glass, containing clean water, without first emptying out the dirty water?"

What is the answer?

Well, all we need to do is place the glass of dirty water under a tap of clean running water. The glass will start to overflow with water, flushing the dirty water out, diluting it and eventually it will be entirely replaced with clean water. Our minds are just the same.

Often we are holding thought patterns that are not clean. Our patterns of thinking can be negative and our negative actions can then reinforce this pattern through repetition. If we see our negative tendencies as being the dirty water that needs to be cleaned out, we can understand how it can be possible to re-programme our thinking by using this analogy.

We cannot get rid of all our old memories by tipping them out. What needs to happen is to add fresh, clean thoughts to our mind. These will then fill the mind and intellect, effortlessly pushing out any negativity and eventually cleaning our consciousness from the inside out.

Then our mind will only be left with thoughts that are in line with its natural state of purity, peace, love, joy and truth. This is the method to transform our thinking.

The Example of Chocolate

Constant attention on our decision-making ability needs to be our main focus. It's the decisions that we make that will lead to either our happiness or our discomfort.

Meditating or reflecting on, "I am a soul," gives power to the intellect as it crystallises the original qualities of love, peace, happiness, purity and wisdom.

Chocolate is a good example to use to observe our patterns or habits. As children, maybe we were given chocolate as a treat, or it is shared in a family or group when they get together. The memory or the experience of being together and the feeling of having fun and being treated, together with the taste, texture, sweetness and enjoyment after eating it, are stored as a memory or sanskar within the soul. Maybe an overall experience of contentment is remembered.

So when we become a little down and need cheering up we think, "I know, what I need is some chocolate." This is then connected to the memory and the experience of being treated, or being in a group having fun or the feeling of contentment, and the association is made internally when we eat it. Fine.

But what happens when we are down for a long time or are regularly down? This habit of eating chocolate for comfort can become powerful and can get out of control, and start to cause problems, as well as having an impact on our health.

We are then being controlled. Not by the chocolate, but by the sanskar.

OK, I know, chocolate is not so bad. But what if it is alcohol, smoking, sleeping tablets or an addiction to drugs, anger or violence? The same principle applies.

What if it's an addiction to negative thinking, low self-esteem, low self-values or destructive behaviour?

These are also sanskars, which can be triggered off at any time, trapping and controlling us, eventually becoming our personality and so our character!

There's a Hole in my Bucket

Thoughts are constantly being created within our minds. This is normal, but they affect our daily energy levels, which then make us feel tired.

How?

Well, imagine that every thought that is created uses up part of the total amount of energy that we have each day, just as the bus has a finite amount of fuel in its tank.

'Driving' my mind in the right direction is the quickest way to get to where I want to be. If I am thinking in the wrong direction, I am using up unnecessary energy or fuel, the same way that the bus uses up diesel unnecessarily if I drive it in the wrong direction or, worse still, get lost! Getting lost is not only uneconomical, but the passengers get pretty upset as well, as they have places to go and things to do, and they can become angry or even aggressive. The body is the same.

Sometimes I can get lost in my thinking or even lost in my mind! When I am driving my mind in the wrong direction, I am wasting valuable fuel/energy and 'I' become tired. Then the body starts signalling to me that energy is getting low, through the experience of pain, tension, stress and irritability. I, the soul, like the driver of the bus can begin to become a little uncomfortable to say the least!

To save this valuable energy, I have to take control of my mind and steer it in the right direction in order to arrive at the right place, at the right time, so avoiding discomfort.

Another issue here is wastage. The bus is wasting precious fuel if the driver drives badly, maybe over revving, heavy breaking or bad choice of gears. This, as well as other mistakes, wastes energy. So, what can happen is that, before arriving at my destination, the bus runs out of diesel and breaks down. Wasteful thoughts do the same thing. Even if I am directing my mind in the right way, I can get side-tracked in my thinking by complaining, comparing or judging. This wastes my energy and, like the bus, eventually leads to a breakdown.

It has been reported that we can produce 40,000 thoughts per day. Even more if we are under pressure or worried! If this is so, each thought that I create is using up part of my overall energy for that day. The more thoughts I have, the weaker each individual thought becomes. There is then a dilution of the amount of power in each thought and each thought is now less effective. This makes me less productive and more tired.

By slowing down my thoughts, each one becomes more powerful. As I am now creating less of them, each thought has more power and can be more easily put into action. The thoughts are now more clean, clear and effective.

How and where can I reduce the quantity of thoughts that I am creating?

These 40,000 thoughts, which are produced per day, can be split into four types – **necessary**, **negative**, **positive** and **wasteful** thoughts.

We need to keep the **necessary** thoughts in order to function, e.g. "I need to open this door before I walk through it."

Negative thoughts are not useful and can be destructive to me as well as to others, so they can go.

Positive thoughts are fine as they help me to enjoy life. They can stay.

Wasteful thoughts, such as thinking about others, comparing myself with others or gossiping, allow my energy to seep away in a non-productive way. They can go as well.

This simple equation can save half the energy available to me each day, which reduces my fatigue or tiredness by 50%. Just slowing down my thinking and observing the quality of my thoughts can easily achieve this.

Practising meditation teaches me how to slow down and become the 'master' of my mind. Each thought is now much more powerful and positive and so more productive. This makes my thinking clearer and I am able to 'catch' situations before they happen, which means that I find myself with fewer problems, less stress and back in control of my life. I am the master of the self-soul.

Such a simple concept and it seems to make sense to me. What do you think?

"Yes, but how?" I hear you say.

Well, I think it needs to be approached in an holistic way. That is to say, this will be the result of changing my attitude and actions in many ways, all of which, I might add, are simple and easy to do, as long as I stay focused on what it is that I want to achieve.

If I really do want to change my habits or personality in a positive way, it's at the thought level that I am going to need to tackle it.

Influences

There are a few areas of our lives to take into consideration when approaching a holistic change. As we have said before, whatever I put into my mind and body is what will come out, well not exactly, but what I put in influences my behaviour. How is my body and mind affected by the activities that I do during the day?

With awareness and understanding, I can steer my life like the bus in the right direction and so be the creator of my own experience. I begin to become the 'designer' of my life, rather than being subservient to outside influences.

Often, people can influence us, either within our family or in the work place, and this may be due to their actions, opinions or their attitude. The expectations of others or our desire to please are another way that we are influenced into acting a certain way. The environment or location we find ourselves in can influence us, as can the atmosphere or vibration of a place. We can be influenced by our wants or desires for possessions, people or places. Our old belief systems can also impact our ability to be influenced.

Media is a powerful influence. I once saw a billboard advertisement showing an M16 machine-gun next to a

TV camera and the caption said, "Which is the more powerful weapon?"

Have you ever noticed that newspapers are 90% bad news? Or that sometimes it's hard to tell if you are watching fact or fiction when you turn on the TV? Anger, violence and fear are instruments of both film-makers and news reporters, and are used to catch our attention in order to boost their viewers or sales.

The Internet is full of adverts, pop-ups and links to divert our attention away from our true self and on to sites to buy stuff that we don't even need! Social networking sites lead us into unnecessary complications and we see adults, as well as youngsters, being trapped by this to varying degrees.

So the trick is to find the balance. Balance is 'stability', which I always used to think was boring and dull and I would constantly choose the highs and always have to experience the lows after. This roller coaster ride of highs and lows can be fun for a while, but imagine if you were on it all day, from the time you woke up to the time you went to bed, and it even continued while you were asleep! This can be the feeling when we are living from a body-conscious perspective.

Experiencing soul consciousness was my wake-up call. A balanced and even lifestyle is a good foundation to build relationships and experience the fullness of life, in harmony with ourselves and others. This is a much safer way of living and it can all start just by being soul conscious. So the trick is - find the balance.

Company

The company that we keep changes throughout our life. By the middle, we can begin to recognise this and, with experience, move towards like-minded people with whom we may have things in common. In this way, we are easily able to relate or communicate with those around us. This is one of the reasons why we gravitate to different groups in society such as clubs, teams and faiths.

When crossing a river, it is said, "Good company takes you across and bad company makes you drown." A bit harsh I know, but it's a good analogy for a physical as well as spiritual way of looking at the way we can be influenced by those around us. The company we keep - and I don't mean just the people but also the places, possessions, ideas, words, attitudes and thoughts inside - is the very thing that can take us across a situation to safety and freedom or can trap and drown us.

Extreme caution and awareness are required. Someone or something can influence us very easily - and it only takes a second! Being soul conscious is my best chance to approach any situation because, if I can hold this awareness, I am able to see the truth from the false and know the right from the wrong in a natural and easy way. I am able to think with conscience and discern the best action to be taken.

The Actors on
the World Stage

One way of dealing with the complications of life is to detach from it while still being inside it. It sounds impossible to do these two things at once, as they seem to be opposites. However, there is a tactic that I have been using for a while that is helpful to overcome this. I think of myself, or consider myself, to be an actor playing a part in a movie.

This life that we are in is the 'ultimate movie' and it's of the highest budget ever possible. In this movie, I can both watch and also play my part at the same time. I see others also acting out their parts, perfectly. All are reading the lines of their script and acting as best they can. I just need to remember that this is like a movie or a play, and then I can really enjoy whatever comes, because it's just a drama. I, the soul, am acting through this costume (the body) within this particular scene that is in front of me.

As an actor, I know that I am separate from my role, that I am a guest playing this particular character, within the film. A guest owns nothing of the place that he finds himself in and so can lose nothing either. This is quite reassuring as I cannot lose, but can only 'win'.

Whether the character that I am playing is successful or a failure, I am always a winner, separate from the temporary part that I happen to be playing at this particular time. Hey presto, freedom. Nice.

As a guest, I am also a trustee, not only of the things around my role, but also of the body/costume itself and I also need to take good care of it. Life now becomes a game and much more fun as the heaviness of identifying with that costume is reduced or even removed. I become free to express myself naturally. The drama plays on and I participate with lightness and loving detachment, enjoying the game, watching each scene unfold with enthusiasm and interest. Now I am really enjoying myself and looking forward to the next episode as well.

Understanding
Relationships

It is often said that, "Two halves make a whole." However, this is not necessarily true when it comes to relationships.

If I am half a circle, constantly looking for the other half in order to make myself whole, I am setting myself up for disaster. Even if I do find the other half and I feel whole, my happiness is dependent on the other half always being there. Dependency is not a healthy way to build a relationship. The laws of nature say that at some point you will be separated and human nature says that at some point you will feel like you need a change (the seven year itch and all that).

What happens when the other one is no longer there, for any number of reasons? I have learnt this the hard way.

In fact, I felt almost whole before getting married, but over time I actually gave away my identity or independence to my partner without realising it. I became dependent on her for many things, support, strength and emotional stability, as well as general organisation of worldly and household matters, like bills and banking, washing and cooking, not to mention entertainment and sex. I handed over my authority to her as a commitment to our relationship gradually over a period of time and I hadn't even realised it was happening.

I really had fallen in love and it feels so great to be in love. Each day was a wonder; the birds seemed to be singing all the time. Everything was rose-tinted with beauty and I never wanted to be separated from my beloved even for a second, as that would have been too long. I would look forward to every time we met and would have butterflies just before the meeting. I was only concerned about being in her company and everything else seemed just unimportant.

However, this feeling lasted for a few fleeting months, or maybe a year at tops, before the relationship became routine and ultimately a bit of a power struggle. As the years rolled by, the lines of communication and things we had in common seemed to break down and dissolve, as each one began to no longer consider the other's feelings or opinions quite so much, until eventually I resigned myself to the fact that we were mismatched. Without expressing it, we both felt trapped and couldn't see any possibility of a future together. The partnership continued to run out of habit for a while but I was 'lonelier' there, in that situation, than at any other time in my life. Bound in a web of karma (actions and interactions), expression suppressed and with no hope of a solution, we went on with life as a 'couple'. I was moving gradually towards the spiritual, minimal side of life and Tami more into the material, fashion, society lifestyle.

Our daughter came along round about that time which breathed a breath of fresh air into our predicament. Like a sparkling star appearing in a dark void, this tiny person reawakened a deep awareness of unconditional love and nurturing. This fresh new member arriving into the family held us together by becoming the focal point for physical and emotional support and sustenance, but really underneath we still had no more in common than the fact that we shared the same surname and resided at the same address.

After a brief move overseas to Portugal, Tami left. I knew it was coming, but it still hurt like mad. False pride, ego and dependency led me to a low I had never felt before. I would say that it took about 2 years to get over her. In hindsight, I can see that I must have been a nightmare to live with, being on such a strange and mysterious journey of inner transformation like a caterpillar mutating into a chrysalis-type creature, while on the outside still stuck in the old habits of desire and self-satisfaction.

I don't blame her at all for leaving; I probably would have done the same in her situation! At the time I was bitter and confused and found it hard to recover from this blow to my identity. It had to happen, to release both of us from a broken and increasingly awkward marriage. Falling that low was the best thing that could have happened to me, although it didn't feel like that at the time.

Now I realise that there is benefit in everything, as I have become a free spirit once again and, at the same time, have the opportunity to have an amazing relationship with my beautiful daughter Ella and a chance to play the role of father/friend. Sometimes I wonder if the whole relationship with Tami may have been just for that, not for us to stay together till old age, but to learn about life and to bring another soul into this world in order to experience itself through a body.

The divorce was surreal. I wondered how, in that civil courtroom, that we could have ever been so intimate and trusting with each other, sharing such joy together. However, I was able see through the 'scene and scenery' and the emotion of that day that Tami did not want to hurt me, but had been influenced by those around her to set legal boundaries in place in order to secure a permanent future without me.

After the separation I approached other relationships in the same selfish manner, just wanting to satisfy my desires and needs as I continued to search for truth. Such a paradox. This was a deep habit/sanskar which had developed over time and repetition from my late teens, and I again fell into repeatedly playing the same role with different partners and making the same mistakes. Over and over again, I re-enacted my script, until finally I understood I really had to change; change my attitude, aim and behaviour. Now and for more than a decade, and I really can't believe it myself, I have been practising a life of celibacy, through choice. That is pure thoughts, pure words and pure actions. This is the result of determined effort that I felt necessary to make in order to have the chance to change my ways permanently.

Why?

Well, for me, my aim now is to clean the soul. To clean the soul, so it can become an 'instrument'. So it can be useful. The intention is to become a world server, one who is a benefactor to other people and the behaviour is now in line with this aim. Life is now simple, clean and uncomplicated. The 'carefree' nature that comes with it reminds me of how I was before puberty, almost childlike and innocent.

I have no regrets about the earlier times. With 'good wishes' and 'pure thoughts', I often send positive vibrations to my daughter and her Mum, seeing them as my sisters and wishing them well for their future. The relationships are now better than ever and I spend plenty of time in the company of my daughter. Thanks to the drama for setting me free – and I mean that from the bottom of my heart.

Another character who had a big influence on me during that time was Kall. I looked to him as a kind of guide and he seemed to fit the bill. He would always try to push the limits, which I liked, but I could never quite keep up with his insatiable appetite for narcotics. He was the best man at my wedding and godfather to Ella. However, he went a bit too far in the 'druggy' world. I would smoke 'joints' after a big night out until I fell asleep, whereas he would use 'harder' solutions. I just couldn't go that far. Again the 'programme' or 'part' recorded in the soul just wouldn't allow me to go that far. I just felt sorry for him, as I watched him fall. Kall still comes into my dreams every now and then, even to this day. Amazing the impact some souls can have on us.

Our Family, Friends
and Connections — Karma

By the middle of life, we have built an incredible network of karma (actions and interactions). This is all part of our journey and the way that we get to know ourselves. Others become a mirror in which we can see ourselves and, thereby, really know ourselves.

My understanding is that we are born into a particular family for a reason. In fact, everything is for a reason, nothing is by chance. The world drama, in which we are actors, is perfectly synchronised.

Karma, which simply means actions, is the 'glue' that holds everything together. This is cause and effect. "What goes around comes around," "As you sow, so you shall reap," "Treat others, as you wish to be treated." Most of us have heard these sayings before. Karma is the reason why everything is the way it is.

As I start to understand the law of karma as a detached observer, I can begin to understand and accept the world as we know it today. I realise that nothing stays the same on the physical plane and that energy starts in its highest form and gradually loses its power as time passes. Matter itself starts in its highest form when it is new and continues to deteriorate with age/time. This is called 'entropy' and is a spiritual law as well as a scientific law.

Note – God is outside this law, as the law of entropy operates within a closed system, i.e. the physical universe, and the Supreme resides outside of this system in the element of spiritual light.

Consider this: our karma is not only from this present experience or lifetime, but can run like a thread through many lifetimes until it is finally settled and zeroed out. It's like paying off a loan that has come to its end after 25 years. There is the final instalment and then it is finished, as long as I don't take out another loan. Understanding karma can help me to see how life may look mighty unfair on the surface and can be difficult to accept if it is observed in one 'time frame'. Otherwise, how else can we possibly understand why some people are born into poverty and others into wealth? Or how some are always healthy, whereas others are sick? Or why one is born into one country or family and another somewhere else?

If you can open your mind to the possibility that, as eternal souls, we are on a journey through human experience, life begins to make much more sense and seems much less unfair. Remember, as I am sure that you can already see, the world is at its most 'unbalanced' at this time, so situations and events can look grossly unfair. From a soul conscious point of view, I am able to see further than just the present and begin to see the bigger picture, that of eternity. This is very useful.

Our present experience now is a direct result of our past actions. Look at education. When a student is at University, she knows that she will pass her examinations by studying and find a good and well-paid job in the future. That future income will be the direct result of her present actions, her studies.

Equally, a bank robber knows that if he gets caught whilst stealing from a bank, he will have to face the consequences and serve his time in prison, so paying off the actions that he performs now.

The economic downturn or 'credit crunch' of 2008 is another example of karma. In the past, the financial industries of the world have acted in a non-ethical way, offering too much money to too many people who simply could not afford it. This credit given in the past is now affecting the economies of the entire world and so the credit crunch is the karmic return of the actions or the decisions made many years ago.

Happiness and love also work in the same way. If I want to be loved, I need to create the return of it, by giving love now. If I donate happiness and make others happy, I will become happy in the future as well as in the present moment.

Lifestyle, and the way I live now, will influence my health in the future. If I treat my body with respect and give it what it needs, i.e. food, exercise and good care, in the future it will accommodate me, rather than break down like the bus that is badly driven.

Nature is also returning the account of the way that we have been treating the Earth over the last 100 years; this comes in the form of natural calamities, such as earthquakes, tsunamis and fires. This is the karmic return from the very elements themselves - earth, water, fire etc. As we have become more out of balance with our desires, the Earth, our home, has become out of balance and is showing us that we need to change our approach to living or we will experience more and more upheaval.

Understanding this helps me to create my future in the present moment. On this level, I am designing my life according to the actions that I perform now. Don't forget, action starts out life as a thought, which is created from an attitude and a feeling. Can you start to see the responsibility we have for our thoughts?

"Whatever I put out, will come back to me." This may not happen immediately, but for sure it will at some point. Perhaps next week, next year, ten years from now or even in my next birth! This principle works on all levels, whether on the level of money, trust, love, peace or happiness. It also helps me to be responsible for my actions as I realise that I will receive the return of those actions. My present experience is a direct result of my past actions.

This is all well and good, and works for this present lifetime to a degree, but what about my actions from any past experiences. I can't even remember them, so how can I repair them? This question brings us back to the power of meditation. Meditation or connection with the Divine transcends time and space. It is the healing power that can repair our past mistakes or the negative actions that we performed. This then clears our karmic accounts, so 'zeroing out' negativity within the soul.

The Hidden History of the Throat

Sometimes, a past action can manifest in the next experience of the soul in its next body. This is one of my karmic accounts and has been on-going for as long as I can remember. It has been a driving force in my understanding and a motivating energy that has been unparalleled on my spiritual journey. This lesson taught me gratitude, hope, acceptance, forgiveness and the lightness of letting go, as well as the self-empowerment of taking responsibility for my thoughts, words and action.

Since childhood, there has been a feeling of constriction in and around my throat area. In early years, as a fairly placid child without too much anger, I would reach a state of panic within seconds if anyone were to touch or hold onto my neck. The very thought of it would cause a disproportionate reaction to what was actually happening in real life. There seemed to be no reason or logic, no rational sense to these responses or reactions to any sort of restriction to the neck area. Together with that would come fear and immediate retaliation towards others.

As time moved on and I grew older, the feeling did calm down, but left a residue of tension and tightness around the tongue and voice box region, leading to a lack of confidence to speak out, due to the amount of effort that was needed to relax and release this part of the body. Realising that there was something not quite right, the soul somehow compensated for this by adjusting and altering the character and the way of speaking accordingly. I would avoid certain situations and circumstances, in order to defend or protect myself from the possible danger of having to face these events. After a while, this became a sanskar. The sanskar, of avoidance of these potential situations where discomfort would be experienced, became a habit and my nature.

This became a serious limitation, one that held me back many times and continued for years. However, it also acted as a motivating energy or drive to find a way to solve the problem, or at least try to understand why it was there. It was this drive that sparked my quest for knowledge. Initially, it was knowledge to heal the body, then to heal the soul and finally knowledge to heal the world. Funny that.

Looking back to those times, I can see that there really is benefit in everything, even the most uncomfortable tensions that we hold in the body! The search for freedom from this discomfort and tension started externally, by using marijuana to relax the whole body. Smoking dope then became a habit, a sanskar, and didn't heal the problem, but probably increased it! Healing and 'therapies' were next and, during that period, I would find that the tension would diminish during a treatment, but would then come back soon after once any element of stress or tension was experienced. Meditation helps very much to relax the body in general and can help with other complaints about health. It conveniently replaced the smoking and of course is completely free and always available.

Although the throat issue was still there, it was now located in quite a specific area having moved directly to the tongue and communication chakra. I continued to observe this condition, as well as searching out possible solutions and people who might be able to help. Eventually I stumbled across a psychic lady who was able to shed some light on the matter.

There was a little misunderstanding about the time of our appointment, so I waited a few hours before eventually meeting Joan, the spiritual healer recommended to me by a friend. The small first floor flat near Paddington train station adjacent to London's West End where she practised her healing was both homely and mysterious. It had a kind of old-fashioned English décor, yet it somehow reminded me of a doctor's surgery. Joan herself, a lady of slight frame in her late fifties, seemed very distant from this world and I wondered how on earth she managed to get anything done. Her manner was gentle and concerned, while a little awkward and forgetful, and her floral dress and cardigan smelt of incense. She had an air of 'knowing', as if she was an authority in something mystical, yet spoke with great humility.

I had prepared some background notes concerning the history of the throat condition to give to her before we started; this included the reason for my visit and the results that I was looking to achieve from the session as well as symptoms, time scales, events and frustrations caused by the ailment. She used a small crystal pendulum with remarkable accuracy, a method called 'dowsing', to uncover any health issues. She used it in the way a surgeon might use a stethoscope. After asking a few questions on general health, she set to work dangling a tiny crystal over different parts of my body. I had asked her to work on the specific problem that had been with me since childhood.

The session was both dramatic and dynamic.

Once she had found the problem, she set about correcting it through 'energy tapping' or EFT which I was already familiar with through a course of videos I had been studying. Emotional Freedom Technique releases energy blockages that can occur during past traumas.

 During this process, my body once again went through many convulsions that led to a great deal of stretching and contorting of the throat and tongue area. Fascinating. Especially the pressure and cries that came out of my mouth, which it seemed, were not instigated by me. This was becoming a 'pattern' that emerged whenever I visited a healer and I was finally about to understand the reason why!

She was able to see the cause of the problem and, after the session, explained what she had seen. This was later confirmed when speaking to my mother about what she had reported. The reason that I was having this issue with the throat was a result of my birth, the way I had been born. As you know, we can't remember being born and for that I am grateful after I found out what she had seen! What she told me made exact sense and I immediately resonated with it.

Apparently she said, I had had a very long and difficult birth and did not seem to want to come into the world. The umbilical cord was wrapped around my neck and was cutting off my air supply. The birth was quite dramatic and extreme.

"The pressure of the cord being around your neck," she said, "caused an energetic imprint on your windpipe and, although the cord is not there now physically, the imprint is still restricting the throat to such a degree that the trauma of the incident is still affecting you to this very day."

Funny how that incident at birth, over 40-years ago, has shaped my whole life experience and was connected to the way I speak, breathe and behave. Amazing! I understood immediately as I had been trying to get my head around 'why' for years. This was part of my karmic account, the account of my past actions, and I am sure that it spanned back further than this lifetime and had a different 'root' even than the birth scenario that she had seen!

After this amazing session, Joan asked me if there was anything else I wanted to heal and jokingly I said, "I think I was shot in a previous life," as I have a bullet-shaped scar from the operation that I had had aged 20, caused by the punctured lung, when the operation had gone a bit wrong.

She looked at me with a deadpan face and said, "No, it wasn't a bullet, it was a spear." I must admit, this shocked me a little, especially when she told me that there had been two spears! The other one had entered through the side of my face, through my nose. This would explain the reason why my sinuses had always been blocked on the right side for as long as I can remember.

I was also curious when she asked if I would like to go back to the incident that she spoke of and clear the energy blockage.

"Of course," I said, without thinking.

Joan explained how, in another incarnation as a settler, I had taken land that was not mine from a tribe of Native American Indians. A battle had taken place, the result of which was that two spears had penetrated my body from different directions. The places that they entered, the lungs and the nasal passages, were the health issues that were still being resolved, a couple of births later, now. The healing continued through more energy tapping and 'forgiveness and acceptance' became the antidote to this long and mysterious condition.

As she seemed to regress me back to that battlefield scene, I became aware of the wrong actions that I had taken. A picture, in the form of feelings and emotions, appeared in my mind and I was able to perceive both the sadness of the tribesmen and my own sorrow with remarkable clarity, although I experienced no actual physical pain. I could see in a very obvious way how my past actions had been affecting my present experiences and that this was caused directly by this incident from the past that was still stored in my unconscious mind.

I was extremely grateful for her help to uncover these mysteries, while at the same time being given a big lesson in karma. However, I also now realised that I needed to 'absolve' my own karma or past negative actions myself in order to settle those accounts permanently and that this could only be done through meditation, connecting to the Source. Otherwise, the treatment would only be for a temporary period and I may also increase my account of karmic 'debt' with the soul that is doing the work for me.

Although the tension in the throat was cleared and felt fantastic, it was short-lived. It returned once again and continues its course until such time that my karmic account is finally settled. I also realised that it is not so helpful to go back into our past lives, as we may have to relive some extremely painful emotional experiences, but rather it's better to look forward to our future. We can create our future according to the actions that we perform now. This is more beneficial. I cannot change my past as it is already over.

Taking everything into consideration, it was still a wonderful insight into the drama, whichever way you look at it. I don't regret it, but I definitely would not do it again!

Can you imagine how complicated and synchronised this game is that we are playing? The funniest thing of all is that we have forgotten the most important factor of all. We have forgotten that we are souls, having a temporary human experience, and we think that we are just these perishable bodies. It's crazy really. The trick is now to, "Consider yourself to be a soul." Become soul consciousness in action.

All of our friendships, family, connections, work colleagues etc., are part of this web of action and interaction. The point of the game is to play, but with awareness and lightness. It is to learn, wake up to our truth, realise that the connection of the self-soul and others with the Supreme Soul is that of 'children' with the 'One Divine Parent'. That is, the perfect Parent. This is enlightenment, lighting-up with knowingness and realisation. I find it fascinating that, even when we become enlightened, we still have to do the washing up or have to drive a bus, but our total experience changes once we are 'awake' with this awareness. There is joy at the feel of the warm water and the soap suds on the hands during the washing up, and delight at the movement of the steering wheel and pedals while driving. It's like seeing behind the scenes and scenery of a drama and just performing each action, role and task for name's sake, but remaining connected to the Source of all love, peace, happiness and contentment, constantly.

Enlightenment... nice.

Competition and Conflict
versus Co-operation

The impact and conditioning of competition may be responsible for many of the conflicts that we experience today. These conflicts start off internally through comparison with others, and can manifest through aggression and even violence as our ego tries to defend itself at any cost. The one that always pays the highest price during these conflicts is the self, the soul.

I used to enjoy playing chess. It's a game of great strategy and is extremely competitive and complicated. Yes, you can play it on a simple level, but, if you really want to win, you need to 'read' the game ahead of the present position on the board. This involves making many internal calculations and the mind and intellect can be stretched to their limits in trying to find solutions. Many calculations of different possibilities are needed, especially if you don't know the 'set piece moves' in order to gain position.

People used to play postal chess; maybe they still do, but maybe now with the Internet etc. Postal chess is when two players, in different places or even different countries, have their Chess board set up in the same way. They make a move and post the co-ordinates of the move that they have made on their board to their opponent, who then resets his board accordingly and does the same, sending a letter back stating his latest move to his opponent by post. As you can imagine, it takes a very long time, weeks or perhaps months or even years, per game. I've never tried this, but even playing an opponent in the normal way, in the same location, can take five or six hours.

Can you imagine what it feels like to lose after such a long time and such intensity of this battle of minds?

Each one is trying every tactic to destroy his opponent, sacrificing pieces, trapping others, luring and plotting, scheming and tricking his enemy into a weak position, in order to go in for the kill, "Checkmate!" Checkmate, is the phrase declared as you win the game. Winning can also happen by forcing the other one to concede.

Needless to say, I don't play chess anymore; it's just too harsh! You begin to 'hate' your opponent and try to deceive him, hoping he won't notice. You set up 'decoys' and divert his attention to other attacks, while going for the jugular.

This is how competition works; it starts off nice and friendly and then becomes nasty and evil, all in the name of winning. Note: EVIL = to LIVE backwards. Competition 'divides' and encourages deception in its extreme. This is called 'tactics', but it's using negative force on the opponent, causing conflict and a struggle or fight on some level.

Sport is similar. It seems harmless enough, just a bit of fun, but leads to division or separation of two or more groups, which leads to false identification with one side. This leads to further conflict and sorrow, victory and defeat, a winner and a loser.

Let's face it; no-one wants to be a loser now, do they?

The law of karma says that whatever I do to someone else will be done to me. I am actually doing it to myself. With this understanding, by wanting to win and make someone else a loser, I am actually making myself a loser in the process.

Check, how do you feel as you read this section?

Can you feel your ego biting? If there is any feeling of 'resistance' to this Universal Spiritual Law, then I have identified with my own desire to win at the price of someone else losing.

This is also how nations operate and how wars take place. It's all due to competition, "I'm better than you," and the actions that need to be taken in order to prove this. This then causes pain, suffering and death on a mass scale, all because of competition.

It's built into our society and into every individual. This is total body consciousness. By competing, we seal our own fate. As a soul, I am connected to every other soul, as brothers. It is 'co-operation' that is needed, not competition.

There is enough food, water and resources on this planet, but yet more than 20% of the world is starving and has no clean water to drink.

Competition... nice?

Football is a good example.

As a kid, from the age 10-15 years, I use to watch football with my Dad. I would play football on a Saturday morning for Sparrows FC and we would generally lose in the early years at least 6-0, but as we took it more seriously in later years we would win many games, even winning Cups. Then in the afternoon we would go to watch the team Dad had followed since he was a boy. I enjoyed the excitement of the crowd and the energy, especially when our team, Crystal Palace, would score a goal. It's an amazing feeling to be in a crowd of up to 50,000 people, which is the largest I remember, and to see your team score a goal. There would be a build-up of energy as the team got closer to the goal area and then a brief drop in noise as everyone holds his or her breath with anticipation, then, "WAHHHHHH, GOOOOAAAALLLL!" A rush of energy as the ball hit the back of the net. There would be a surge of happiness as 30,000 home-team fans literally jumped into the air and screamed, throwing their arms skyward. Nice, I loved it; and just wished that they would score more often!

Now, the downside is that, when they didn't score or, even worse, when they lost, which seemed to be quite regularly for our team, the equivalent sorrow would be experienced and a dark cloud would descend into the car on our way home from the game. Not nice.

It is highs and lows again, but, mainly, unfortunately, lows. It is 'them' against 'us'. "If you're not with us, then you're against us." The 'fans', that's short for 'fanatics', identify with their teams so much that they actually feel pain if their team loses. "It's only a game," I would think, "what's the point of losing your happiness?"

The fans all wear the same colours, buy the same scarf and hat of their team and, if they see the other team's fans, they fight with them. This was quite shocking to me as a child and very violent back in the 1980s. People would get hurt and there would be blood, and all for the sake of a game. So much aggression to other human beings, just because of the colour of their shirt, hat or scarf. Disregard for life and no respect for others' point of view; I just didn't get it.

Now look at countries. It is the same. They fight over 'invisible' borders placed by politicians, over the colour of their flag and the culture of their people.

When there is competition, there is always division. When there is division, there is always conflict. The very root of conflict is competition and we are taught to be competitive from a very early age by society and parents.

Whenever there is a winner, there is always a loser.

Co-operation makes so much more sense. Why not create win-win situations?

Competition is the certain equation:-

Over-identification + Defensiveness + Aggression + Hysteria

= Sadness + Sorrow

= Pain + Loss, for all involved.

When nations compete, there is always a high cost, both economically as well as ethically. Nations condition their inhabitants to be loyal and to fight for their country, but at the same time manipulate them through social and financial control, treating them as if they are just numbers.

We can observe that it's often the 'few' making the decisions for and controlling the many. Sometimes it's not even for the benefit of the nation, but for their own greed, power and desires.

Competition, nice?

Detached Observer
- Loving and Detached

Is it possible to be both loving and detached at the same time?

This is a highly misunderstood concept. People think of 'coldness' when you use the word 'detachment', but, as with many spiritual words and phrases, we are trying to use physical words to explain a spiritual experience, which is of course non-physical. Words are coloured or loaded by the past experiences that we associate with them. The word father may mean something loving and supportive to one person and a tyrant to another. Yet we have to use some sort of bridge to understand these spiritual aspects so the words that we use can lead us into a spiritual experience through feelings.

The only way I can be truly loving is to be detached.

It seems harsh I know, but I realised a while ago that everything I try to hold on to with love, I would lose, for it is love that lets go. When I can let go with love, that thing or person will come back naturally. This seems to be another Spiritual Law. It is only fear that holds on.

This is the challenge for many parents. Some are not able to let go of their children when they leave home, and somehow lose their sense of purpose and meaning when this happens. In this case, happiness is based on something external, outside of them, and so it can be taken away at any point. I experienced this first hand, when custody of my daughter (I don't mean that I own her, it's just a way of explaining the relationship between us) was given to her mother, rather than jointly. It was as if my heart had been ripped out. This is a classic example of my attachment to another human being at that time. 'Big Lesson', but one that I am very pleased I have learnt, as I will not connect my identity or happiness to anything physical and outside of me like that again. It's just asking for trouble really!

Being a 'detached observer' in situations has shown me that I can be in a scenario or situation and see that whatever is happening is happening only on a physical level. Yet, I the soul don't have to be affected by it. I just have to remain detached and loving while living my own life.

No-one can do anything to me, unless I allow them to.

No-one can make me angry unless I allow myself to become angry.

No-one can hurt me, the soul, unless I allow them to.

The question is, "How do I want to feel?"

My answer is always going to be 'happy'; therefore I must not let anyone ever take away my happiness. It's up to *them* what they do and I cannot always stop that, but it's up to *me* not be affected by those actions and lose my inner state of happiness.

One way of dealing with this is to understand that there is a difference between the soul and the actions that it performs. If I am able to separate these, I can then judge the action performed for rightness, while not judging the soul. This is useful as I can then forgive much more quickly and not hold on to bad feelings or grudges that may have happened in situations of the past and continue to affect me now. Also, I am not creating or sustaining a bad atmosphere. I can then allow the past to be the past, learn from it and remain free and in the present, not trapped by constantly worrying about something that happened 10 minutes ago, 10 weeks ago or 10 years ago.

In this way, I am freed from past events and able to enjoy the present moment. After all, a present is a gift. I can then see the bigger picture and become more accepting of people, situations and events which would have upset me before. With this skill, I can design how I want to feel. I respond to events and do not live a life of reaction.

Silence versus Science

Maturity has given me an understanding of the external and the internal.

Science is connected to the external, whereas silence is our original internal quality and form. Silence used to scare me and I would always fill every moment with people, sounds, actions and activities. It was just a distraction that I was creating and now I realise that I was sabotaging myself. It's only when I give myself space for silence and stillness that magic can happen. Filling every moment with stuff stops me from 'being', and I end up just a human doing, rather than a human being.

In silence, allowing my body and mind to remain still, I am able to catch the subtle vibrations of the self, the Divine, and the divine energies gently guiding and directing me. This in turn, brings truth and lightness into my internal world. From this foundation of silence, I can fulfil my role as a positive influence on my surroundings or, you could even say, a transformer of negative energy and an ambassador of light.

Silence is not just as in 'not speaking', although this is a good place to start. When I have spent time practising silence for a few days, I have experienced a change in awareness. Silence of the 'mouth' enables me to re-centre my thoughts, not constantly having to formulate sentences, conversations and answers. Remaining silent brings a sense of freedom, liberation from the ordinary. And let's face it, much of what we speak about is unnecessary and can even be negative. Keeping quiet is a form of safety from being pulled into something that we don't really need to be involved in. It's a weapon of self-defence.

You could say that even having an opinion, that I am attached to, is my ego. By this I mean that, if I want or desire to have a certain outcome from any given event, I put myself in a position whereby, if that outcome does not happen, I may feel upset or angry and react. Ego is so subtle. Ego is defensive. Watch out for it, it will deceive you if you let it!

Once I can slow down my words, the mind also begins to slow down and becomes much more focused and more powerful. Each thought becomes stronger and more potent; the 'chatter' of the mind then begins to calm down. What a relief.

It is said that, "Silence is more powerful than Science." Science relates to the physical and silence is connected to the subtle. More often than not, 'subtle' is more powerful than physical. Maybe this is how to understand that statement. Gravity is a good example of the subtle. You can't see it and are not really aware of it, yet it is the greatest physical force in the Universe. Science looks outside; silence looks inwards. Silence brings me to a state of simplicity and, with that simplicity there is clarity, and wisdom starts to function. Science can lead to expansion and complications.

While spending time in silence, I have realised that words are not only clumsy, but are often misunderstood or misinterpreted. There is a 'cleverness' that comes with words, e.g. saying one thing and meaning another or saying something bitter in a sweet way. Sarcasm and criticism can also be mixed in. This creates bad feeling, not only in the one speaking, but also in the one hearing, and the entire atmosphere is then spoilt.

I find that silence is useful when some space is needed, either within a conversation or in order to dilute a heated situation or argument. This space allows solutions to enter into an otherwise full arena and so conflict can be avoided. Often situations can sort themselves out with a little silence. Remember, we are not talking about 'the silent treatment', but about a few seconds space to send good vibrations to the other person or situation to positively charge the interaction, bringing a bit of lightness to a heavy situation. This space is a chance to connect to the self and emerge the original qualities of the soul - love, peace and happiness - as it also promotes an opportunity to see the other as a being of light, before continuing into the activity. This truly creates a feeling of being soul conscious in action.

The interactions or disagreements that occur with others are the 'acid test' to check our own inner stage of awareness. By observing our own thoughts, feelings and attitudes, we can measure our current position and progress on the spiritual path to confirm that basically it's 'all good'. These tests are sent to us in many shapes and sizes, in all sorts of disguises and forms. To make these tests our friends and to welcome them when they come is to truly realise the soul-self. And to live in this awareness is the most elevated stage a human being can achieve, soul consciousness. Of course, this too is still a stepping-stone to a higher level that can be achieved with practice, that of an Angel.

Peace

Peace is our original state of being; we just need to reconnect to it. It's only when I realise that, "I am peace," and that I don't need to look outside of myself to find it, that I can then begin to experience it. All the time I am physically searching for peace outside, I am looking in the wrong place. If I do find it, it will be temporary and short-lived. When the source of my peace is physically outside of me, I can also be controlled by it. It can be taken away at any point, so that limited peace is also connected to the fear, "What happens if I lose this peace?"

Through meditation, I can emerge my own peace from inside the soul and live from that basis. This realisation is extremely empowering and uplifting. It also enables me to fill up with that peace and donate it to all other beings, the Earth and the elements themselves.

When I know that my original quality is of peace, I can then connect to the Supreme Source of all peace. God, the Divine, is both non-physical and unending, and from Her I can recharge my batteries, by filling up with Her unlimited quality of peace.

Health and Illness

As we are practising soul consciousness, let's have a look at the interaction between the body and soul. I have to keep remembering that I am a soul and this is my body. This is one of the most slippery aspects to catch hold of; it's a bit like mercury, constantly running away! It is one of the main efforts to make, along with remembering to connect to the Source of Divine Energy.

The body grounds the soul into the physical world through the sense organs and nervous system in order to experience, but it is the soul that actually feels. The soul is the eternal identity of who I truly am.

You could even say that the body is non-living and that it is only when the soul enters the foetus at four to five months that the body becomes alive. Up until then the body is just matter without any consciousness, unable to think or feel. Once the soul is inside the baby body in the womb, it begins to influence the growth, shape and form of the matter that it is occupying. The sanskars of the soul, which are carried from any previous records, now influence that tiny body. These sanskars are carried from the past experience, from one lifetime to another, and are played out as characteristics of the soul, which is now in its new body. They then create exactly the experience that the soul needs this time around.

Past karmic accounts are often continued from lifetime to lifetime, in order to settle any outstanding situations or issues that the soul needs to resolve. My feeling is that the soul somehow sub-consciously agrees to and chooses its next set of circumstances in order to continue this and that it just wants a sense of completion of any unresolved past issues. Having originally left its Home of Light and maybe having gone too far off balance in one lifetime, it feels that it needs to rebalance itself in its next life. This may mean living a life that seems unfair on the surface, if observed as a single lifetime on its own. However, in the bigger picture, there is balance, harmony and fairness.

Everything is constantly changing; in fact, the only thing we can be sure of is change.

The soul feels and experiences through the body, but is not the body. The body is made of the five elements, which are temporary and will return back to their source, the Earth, "Ashes to ashes, dust to dust." Energy just keeps transferring. Each time it does so, it reduces in power. The human soul is spiritual, living energy, consciousness and can never be destroyed. It can also never be created. It just 'is'.

Health issues are one way the soul is able to become aware of disharmonies within it and these disharmonies can express themselves through the body in the form of illness. Once identified, damaging patterns or habits can be changed and we can start the process of rebalancing. Health shows us that we may need to change the actions we are performing, as well as the relationship between the soul and its body. Health issues can arise to wake up or jolt the soul back into knowing itself.

Within the physical world, the body is the mechanism for the soul to know itself through. The biggest problem is that we forget that we are this eternal being and that we (the soul) can never die. It's only the body that dies, which is made of the five elements, earth, water, fire, air and space. It is just a temporary vehicle or costume that we are looking after as trustees.

Like the bus, it needs to be maintained nicely and it needs to be kept clean. I have to put fuel in the bus and it needs an MOT every now and then. It needs oil and to be driven, exercised. When I drive the bus, I need to be careful not to hit anything and to treat it with care, otherwise there will be damage. The body is the same. Look at kids and the way they treat their bodies. They think that they are indestructible, but, as they grow older and have injuries or illnesses, they learn to look after their bodies. There can be many repercussions in later life for any damage done in the younger years.

I need to value my body, because it's the vehicle that I use to get around in and to interact with others. I have useful instruments like ears, eyes and a mouth so I can communicate. Legs and arms are handy as well.

If I treat the bus badly, it will wear out quickly, and the body is the same. Ill health is a way of reminding me, the soul, that something is out of balance. If I notice, listen to or see the signs, I can resolve the problems. If I don't, then I will have to pay the price at some point. The body itself doesn't experience any pain. It's the instrument or device which sends messages through the nervous system to the brain to be collected, felt or experienced by the soul. The finger doesn't care if it is cut or broken. It's the soul that has to deal with the pain.

Pain

Pain is the signal that the soul receives when the body or mind is being damaged. It is like the warning lights that are illuminated on the dashboard of the bus for the driver to take action on. The driver has to first of all notice these signals and then he must rectify the problem in order to continue on his journey.

Pain can be compared to these signals on the bus and can be approached on three levels.

1) There is the pain of the now that I experience at this moment.

2) The pain of the past that impacts on me now through my memory of that pain, either physical or emotional.

3) The pain of the future, that has not yet happened but is what I am anticipating or expecting.

If I really want to reduce my pain;

1) I need to put a 'full stop' to the past and not allow it to continually affect me in the present moment.

2) I should forget about the future potential pain, as it hasn't happened yet and might not happen. It's this worry about the future that causes stress and then illness.

Even the present pain can be reduced if I realise that I am a soul, experiencing this through the body for a temporary period of time. Soul consciousness gives me the overview of what is happening and I am able to experience being detached from the pain and watch it come and go.

Ill health can be a door to realisation, a wake-up call to reality or something that I need to change. Or I can say, "Why me?" Then we are trapped in an endless cycle of pain and self-pity.

"As soon as we are born, we start dying."

From a physical point of view, our cells deteriorate all the time and are changing and being renewed constantly. In fact, every cell of the body is replaced over a seven-year period. So, think how old you are and divide that by seven and you will see how many times, 'you-the soul' has replaced the entire matter that 'you-the soul' are sitting in. "Of course we are souls and not bodies, it's obvious."

Creative Visualisation
"Bubbles of Peace"

During the middle of our lives, we can combine the maturity of life experience with the knowledge of the child-like stage of innocence, as by this time we are aware of both. The balance between being the 'master' and the 'child' allows us to remain light, even whilst having responsibilities, and continue to have fun in our adulthood.

This easy visualisation created by a friend of mine can help us to stay carefree while practising the serious task of spreading positive vibrations and good wishes to all souls and to the world. You can try it out on your own, or maybe slowly read it aloud to your family or friends. You will be amazed by their response.

Close your eyes…

Be very still and imagine you are holding a huge bottle of bubble liquid.

You are going to blow some bubbles.

These are special peace bubbles that will drift through the world spreading peace everywhere.

First, become very quiet and peaceful inside…

Take a deep breath and, as you breathe in, feel as if you are breathing in deep peace...

Imagine that you are breathing peace into your lungs and whole body...

Now breathe out peace into the atmosphere...

Breathe in peace... and breathe out peace...

Breathe in peace... and breathe out peace...

Now take your bubble wand and breathe in peace and as you blow out... blow as many bubbles as you can.

Imagine that you are filling each bubble with peace.

Breathe in peace again... and blow peace into the bubbles.

Now watch the bubbles drift upwards into the sky and move along.

Where in the world would you like to send them?

Just have the thought and the peace bubbles will obey and softly land in the place where you sent them.

The bubbles will spread thoughts and feelings of peace to that place...

Spend a few more moments breathing in peace... and blowing your bubbles...

Breathe in peace again... and blow some more bubbles...

Watch as the delicate shining bubbles of rainbow light drift softly through the air.

They are carrying all your thoughts of peace to the places in the world that need peace...

It feels so good, to be sending peace into the world...

Blow your bubble of peace for as long as you wish...

Breathe in peace... and breathe out peace...

Breathe in peace... and breathe out peace...

Observe the difference in the feeling and vibration in the room before and after this Visualisation, and the expressions and awareness of those who participated. This very simple exercise can show us how to change the world from our inside, out.

PART 3

THE END

The end of one thing is always the beginning of something else. It is only when we let go of something that there opens up the space for another thing to come into our life. The end can be the completion of a particular episode. It is a final scene of the play and is when all the actors come on to the stage.

It is an end, or the thought of the end, that can inspire us to change a course of action or an attitude that we have been holding on to.

The end is fulfilling. When we finish a tasty meal, there is a feeling of contentment. When we are watching the end of a film, how do we feel? It is only by reaching the end that we can know the whole of the movie and we don't feel as if we have missed anything.

It is as we reach the end of a situation or event that our full wisdom has been accumulated. The end and wisdom are very much connected together. The phrase 'wise old man/woman' connects experience with wisdom.

The end often brings a sense of comfort once it has been reached, there is nothing left to be done, the journey is complete. Once a task is finished, there can be a feeling of satisfaction as we look back at a job well done. Then we are able to move on to whatever is next.

This last section looks at how our life can be transformed when we end one way of acting and adopt a different way of thinking and being, while in action. I have found that it is a simple switch of our awareness and that it takes just one second to change our attitudes and our lifestyle. One second of remembering who I am and then approaching each day from this new perspective.

What follows are a few personal experiences, stories and insights that may help to inspire a new way of being.

Being Soul Conscious.

The Forest of Honey

The end of my external search for truth was the beginning of my internal journey into that which is genuine, the soul.

After a few amazing experiences whilst meditating, still quite 'green', and almost disbelieving that anything this positive and good could actually exist, I decided that the only way I would know for sure whether this path of Raja Yoga was the right one for me was to go to the source. The source, being the headquarters of the Brahma Kumaris World Spiritual University, is located at the top of a mountain on a plateau area known as Mount Abu, Rajasthan, India.

Could I take this way of living seriously or not? Should I take the plunge?

I had already been to India before and spent a few months travelling around and loved it, feeling that it was my home already. I remember in 1991 landing in Calcutta for the first time, which, by the way is absolutely filthy and covered with slum areas, thinking, "This looks familiar," feeling that, "I should have just come here in the first place," and not worried about all the other countries I had visited on the way. My heart recognised this land.

Anyway, I had been saving up some money to go back to India in 2001 and was in the planning stage when India, quite literally, came to me in the form of Raja Yoga.

Madhuban, which means 'forest of honey', is the name given to the headquarters, and I was drawn to go see it for myself. I knew that to truly get the 'full dose', the full experience, which was to attend a large meeting at the University with over 20,000 students from all over the globe, I would have to 'qualify'. Not qualify as in sitting an exam or winning a race, but that I would have to be prepared, physically, mentally and spiritually in order to maximise the benefit from this opportunity.

This is what I was told: -

> - *You will need to have been practising the principles of the University for a minimum of 8 months.*

> - *You will need to have attended regular classes, in order to understand the teachings and philosophy of the practice of Raja Yoga.*

"OK," I thought, "That makes sense, yes, let me try it."

So attend regular classes I did, and they did help me to understand the many beautiful experiences I was already having during meditation. Fine, now the lifestyle change. This was a bit trickier. I would need to start leading a 'pure' lifestyle.

"What exactly do you mean," I said?

Following a 'Sattvic' vegetarian diet was the first bit - this refers to a yoga diet or sentient diet, and is a diet based on foods that, according to Ayurveda and Yoga, are strong in the sattva guna, and lead to clarity and upeksa (equanimity) of mind while also being beneficial to the body. It is pure food of high vibration, which meant no meat, fish or eggs and no pungent foods, like onion and garlic, as these affect the quality of the thoughts produced in the mind and hamper the meditation.

"OK, fine, I'll give it a go."

The Tunnel of Fear

This 'end' was the end of my long relationship with marijuana and, to tell you the truth, it was quite a relief to be free of that habit.

It was time to stop smoking, drinking and taking mind-altering substances. The main reason for this was to help purify the body and the mind in order to cultivate a spiritual lifestyle through meditation.

This was a little harder, as I had been in the habit of smoking for about 10 years and drinking for more than 18 years. The recreational drugs mainly were not a problem. I was really at the end of that phase anyway and also wasn't mixing with that crowd of people so much.

I'd been trying to change those habits for a while, but just didn't quite seem to have the will power or strength. I say 'mainly' because I did still like to get stoned, smoking marijuana most days. In fact, by this point, meditation was relaxing me in the same way, better even, and without the coughing.

"Anyway," I thought, "I like smoking and I don't really want to stop."

The tobacco, I could take it or leave it, which was easy. I just needed to find a way to continue to get stoned without the tobacco. No problem.

I had been given a small pipe a few years earlier, so I dug it out of a box and used it in the evenings, just to relax. The idea was to use this titanium pipe 'occasionally' so breaking the habit of continuously rolling up and smoking joints. This seemed like a good idea at the time and a good way to begin the process of stopping smoking.

The only problem was that I found that smoking in this way 'occasionally', I would get extremely high. It was quite different from my usual style of smoking. It was quite a heavy, deep 'stone' without the tobacco. Initially, it worked well and I began to wean myself off the habit that I liked, but didn't like, as I felt trapped by my psychological need for smoking and the associated feelings that went with it. Really, I wanted to stop it.

I had been in the habit of smoking for quite some time, and it had always been a very social activity and a support to get through the monotony of everyday life. It was a kind of release from the heaviness of society and life in general. I had relied on it to soften reality and take the edges off things and I couldn't imagine life without it. This is a typical sign of dependency. But the new method was not like this; it was unsociable. In fact you could say even 'antisocial'. One small pipe would send me into a deep 'stone' which would last for about 3 hours. It would start off heavy and powerful, leaving me with vegetable-like numbness in the body and would gradually subside over the following hour or so to a point where I would actually be able to move and walk and talk again.

This experiment in changing my habits only lasted a few weeks, probably because I was meditating and wanted to change for the better. It was then that I had what you could call 'a bad trip'. It wasn't like me to have a bad trip and it scared me into never touching the stuff again, which was a 'blessing in disguise' really, but it sure didn't feel like that at the time.

It all happened one evening on an innocent walk from my flat in the Isle of Dogs in East London through a foot tunnel under the Thames River to Greenwich.

The 'Isle of Dogs', which is very near Canary Wharf - a financial area of London, is surrounded by water on 3 sides from the Thames and, on its fourth side, by a canal which allowed boats to enter into the Wharf itself. This makes it into an island, even though it is located in the centre of London itself.

I will never forget that night.

The tunnel was a pedestrian walkway, which dated back to the times when workers living on the south side would cross the river to work in the shipyards in the early 1900s. I had used this tunnel many times before to visit Greenwich, which is on the south side of the river.

That evening, Hanna, my Portuguese girlfriend, who, incidentally, was a bit of a 'wild chick', and I had been smoking the little pipe before going out, and I was heavily stoned as well as a little paranoid, to say the least. This can happen as you will know if you have ever been stoned. By the time we had reached the tunnel, the full ferocity of the pipe's effects had reached its greatest intensity. Normally, this is the time to be sitting, or even lying down, in a warm and safe environment, not having to deal with any sort of interaction with the world in general. What on earth were we doing 'out' in that state?

The old cast iron stairs spiralled down to a leaky, dirty foot tunnel, which descended downwards on its passage under the river, then turning a little at one point before climbing up again halfway, towards the exit at the other end. There was a strange musty sort of smell in the tunnel, and it was in a state of disrepair with graffiti and rubbish scattered about in the usual urban inner-city style.

My head was cloudy and throbbing with pressure from the marijuana and I staggered along with Hanna while the tunnel echoed with strange and weird sounds. We tried in vain to avoid the many puddles, that would have been hard to navigate even in a sober state, and I remember the walls being covered in mould.

From the tunnel came a booming, blood-curdling sound that, to my dismay, I realised was between us and the other end, which just happened to be our escape route out. Paranoia increased together with a deep disturbance that penetrated my very being, but of course I couldn't show it. "I can handle it." As the tunnel led us under the river, the noises became louder and began to echo more and more, becoming twisted and distorted as the sound waves were amplified in the enclosed environment of the tubular walkway.

"What in God's name could produce such a sound?" I was screaming internally, but remained steady on the outside. We were walking towards what could only be certain death and dismemberment by what must be a 'dragon of the darkest nature'. Or maybe there was an axe-wielding maniac waiting to chop us up into small pieces down there in that tunnel. My imagination was running out of control!

Gradually, as we got closer to this terrifying sound, still not able to see what it could be, I felt like turning and running for my life, but how could I? I would have to be brave and face it. As we continued to walk, it felt like we were on a conveyor belt that was moving in the opposite direction to the way we were facing. This was one of the tricks-of-the-mind due to the high quality 'pollen' that we had smoked earlier in the little pipe.

The sound was tormented and tortured by now, as the acoustics of the tunnel twisted the resonance and increased the volume, adding mid-range frequencies that upset me beyond belief. The sound was now a screaming and babbling wail of unrecognisable words.

"What language could it be?" An unearthly one, that's for sure.

Trembling, we turned the corner and ahead of us was a figure standing in the centre of the tunnel, which was only about 8 feet wide! We would have to walk right up to this monster in order to pass. There was no other option.

"RUN, escape, FLEE while you still can...." anything to avoid the fire-breathing dragon ahead, which we were approaching. By this time, I was beside myself with despair, quivering in my boots, I was doomed. Head still heavy from smoke, senses distorting reality, I nearly vomited with fear right there.

Louder and now more ferocious than ever. There must be some sort of human sacrifice going on just ahead in that tunnel. I nearly did something in my trousers. I became almost frozen in time as we got closer and closer to this demon in the centre of the tunnel. The troll would surely rip off our heads and scoop out our brains. There we stood in front of Hell's Guardian, the Devil himself, Beelzebub, Satan.

At this point, I vowed, "I will never, never, never do it again. I promise not to ever, ever, smoke again if I can just be saved, freed from this nightmare." There was no going back now; we had to face the beast. Our lives were in great danger. We would surely be mutilated and eaten by the creature. The sound of death and warped elongated screeches and squeals continued to thunder all around us. 'It' was just ahead of us now.

That's when it happened.... we glided gently past the... 'busker'...! I was both shocked and overwhelmingly relieved beyond belief as he was now behind us and we were somehow, still alive and heading to the exit of the tunnel. The demon that had been creating this most terrifying of sounds was simply a busker, a musician, with his guitar and an open guitar case to collect enough small change to buy a few beers at the end of the night. He winked and tipped his hat as we escaped towards safety, his guitar, the weapon of mass-destruction, tucked under his arm. That song, compressed by the tunnel and the busker's dark presence and tatty clothes, will haunt me forever.

True to my word, I never did smoke again after that fateful night. It was a turning point and the end of my 10-year love affair with cannabis. That was the last time I went anywhere near the pipe!

Purity

The word purity seems to be misunderstood in the world today and has lost its importance and value.

How can we define purity?

Well, purity is the absence of anything impure. Simple.

For example, if an ice-cold glass of fresh milk has even one drop of poison in it, the whole thing becomes impure and so its purity has finished. The whole glass of milk is then not pure.

Purity is often thought of as 'prudish', but actually it brings back a wonderful sense of innocence, almost like a second childhood. After practising purity in thoughts, words and actions, not just celibacy, for the past 14 years, I can say that it is a joyful, rejuvenating experience. There is a feeling of cleanliness. This is purity, as in lifestyle. Like a child, the 'carefree' lifestyle begins to unfold and any upsets are short-lived. This 'child-like' state is the result of purity.

Towards the end of my external search or 'research', and while I was practising hatha yoga postures and finding it very rewarding physically, mentally and spiritually, a real awakening in regard to lifestyle was taking place. I started to read a book about the benefits of Iyengar Yoga and ways to improve and increase those benefits. I was happily reading away until I arrived at a section towards the back entitled 'Way of Life', some 300+ pages into the book, which disturbed me.

It recommended that a balanced vegetarian diet was helpful. Good. Also, that a positive mental attitude is useful. That's fine. The bit about 'evacuating the bowels' before practising gave me a bit of a chuckle. Fine.

Next, it stated that to really take maximum benefit from this particular form of yoga, celibacy was recommended.

"What?"

"Say it again?"

"Did you say celibacy?"

"Help, no, it can't be." I just couldn't believe it.

"Just when I had finally found yoga, something that was beginning to change my life in a positive way, they tell me that I can't have sex!!"

"Wait a minute, no, this can't be right?"

At that time, which was months before the tunnel incident, I was in a relationship with Hanna and had been for several years. From the time we met in Portugal, our relationship was quite a physical one and we had many things in common from music to parties to well, more parties... Finally having found someone who had a libido as high as mine after years of searching, they now tell me it's best to be celibate!!

"Just my luck," I thought. Talk about a kick in the crotch!

So I skipped that section and carried on reading as if it wasn't there. But it had planted a seed in my mind. I had up until then identified with sex for years and felt that it was very much part of me, if not all of me. Anyway I liked sex, nothing wrong with that 'two consenting adults' and all that. "No harm."

So I tried to put it to the back of my mind and carried on as usual, as if nothing had happened. But it had. Practising Iyengar Yoga knowing that, "I could be better if..." and, "I could improve if..." But yet carrying on, was like lying to myself. It was a cop-out, a con. I started not to take the yoga so seriously any more, just in case I would have to start being celibate.

"No thanks," I thought, but I had been shaken all right. I began to question myself, "What is it that I am trying to achieve?" Is it concentration, attention and realisation, or is it chasing after the opposite sex or trying to find a life-partner? Logically it made sense, but my habits were saying, "No, no and just no."

It was around about this time that the leaflet saying 'Learn how to Meditate for Free' landed in my hand. Strangely, it was Hanna who spotted this 'signpost' and recognised that this was something worth investigating. She was, in many ways, the one who was guiding me along the path, and I still couldn't see it at that time! This was an amazing coincidence (or not?), as it was an opportunity to slightly change direction with my yoga practice.

For a while, the two yoga's ran together hand-in-hand, Iyengar Yoga and Raja Yoga Meditation. Although, after a few months and some wonderful meditation experiences, the Iyengar Yoga just didn't seem as important any more. Reading that book and uncovering ideas that I didn't like had cooled off my intensity and interest in taking it much further.

So my energy was now going into meditation, which was starting to transform my life so quickly that I couldn't believe my luck.

"This is what I have been looking for." I was so excited.

"This is my chance; I've just won the lottery with this meditation thing."

The lifestyle change that stunned me was the next 'bombshell' to hit me.

The final part of the 'pure lifestyle', which it was necessary to be practising in order to visit the Brahma Kumaris Headquarters at Madhuban in India, and attend the huge gathering, was...?

"Celibacy...!"

"Not again."

"What's going on here? It's some sort of conspiracy." I was horrified.

But something inside me knew that I had to face it this time. So I waited and thought about it, and began to ask myself a few serious questions.

"What do I really want?"

"Do I want to be a master of the self or a slave to my habits, mind and desires?" After all, look where it's got me to so far...? Confused, disconnected and without direction... are some of the conclusions that came to mind. I really had to think about this though. Was I really prepared to give up sex? Why should I stop doing what I liked?

So, after some deep thinking, reasoning over a few weeks, I made a deal with myself. "The Universe is trying to tell me something here; I really need to listen to the signals that are being sent to me at this time." I thought, "This is just too much of a coincidence!"

"Ok, I will give up sex for just as long as I need to in order to get to Madhuban. Once I have been there, I will be able to take it up again... Yes, that sounds reasonable." I convinced myself. "I'll do it." I made the commitment, knowing that it wouldn't be easy; I just had to give it my best shot.

Not surprisingly my girlfriend was unimpressed with my decision. I don't think she believed that I would go through with it, that I would have the strength. I remember her saying, "Oh no, not another brother," as she joked about becoming my sister.

So, I began to clean up my act.

I stopped swearing and cussing. It was quite easy really. The sarcasm and cynicism, which were deeper than I had imagined, came next. Not so difficult. I stopped smoking, although it was hard to stop the marijuana until that dragon incident in the tunnel. I stopped drinking straight away. The vegetarianism was a cinch. However, the celibacy was a tough one.

At 34 years old, Hanna wanted a child and had for quite some time considered me as the father of her baby-to-be. This turn of events was going to make it very difficult to achieve that! We had lost one pregnancy a few months earlier and she knew that her body clock was ticking! Respect to her though, as she did give me a chance, probably thinking that I wouldn't be able to maintain it for long and that I'd give in. However, I was determined. Trust me, it was not easy, sleeping in the same bed together, but I had a goal and I knew that I had to give it a try or I would never really know for sure. I just couldn't let this possibility of answers to so many questions pass me by.

To create some space between us in a very gentle way, I began to make myself as unattractive as possible, changing my attitude, intention, manner and even the way I looked. I even grew a beard - not that beards are unattractive, for you beard wearers out there!

She was not a happy bunny and, after a few months, she left.

This was becoming a habit, being left!

It was a sad and lonely day, and I remember waving her off at the Docklands Light Railway station Mudchute, wondering, "What have I done...?"

We remain friends to this day and she did have that child that she always wanted. I wish them both well and still see them every now and then, even though they live in another country.

Hanna was a real catalyst for my transformation. She was a leading light in recognising signals and messages being sent out by the drama. She wanted me to find what I was looking for and for that support I am most grateful. Something inside was driving me to make these dramatic life changes and I just had to go along with it, watching and viewing as an observer. It was a big turning point in my life and I wasn't even sure if I had made the right decision. Single-mindedly, I continued to endure my renunciation while studying and practising the path. I was 'intoxicated' spiritually and felt I was making ground at last in understanding the self and taking control of my physical organs, like a good driver steering the bus on the straight and narrow through the storms of negativity. That is, until she came back to visit after a few months and stayed with me. Tricky.

By now I was into a routine, my spiritual routine. I was making progress and starting to have some mind-blowing experiences. Her visit became quite a challenge. I was doing OK for a week or two, maintaining a bit of distance between us and keeping busy and out of trouble. I realised that she had been emotionally damaged by my decision and had been crying for months. I truly felt mercy for her. I did my best to both comfort her and make myself unavailable to her at the same time.

I tried to transform our relationship from lovers to brothers. I began to practise soul consciousness, to see her as if we were in the same family, which of course we are on a spiritual level. I spoke to her differently, interacted differently and even looked different, just in order to show her that I was not the same person that she had fallen for.

I felt reinvented, redefined and even reborn, and I needed to express this to her. I really didn't want to hurt her, but I needed to heal myself. For a further week or so, the quiet battle of chastity was waged until I became feverish and caught the flu. This added dimension to my 'struggle' shattered my armour; I became weak and needed to take her support momentarily while she nursed me well. That was all it took, the touch; the closeness and the associated memories came flooding back. We made love again and, for the first time in my life, it reduced me to tears. I was sobbing with emotion, emotion that told me this is it, this is the last time.

It was a mixture of sadness, guilt, frustration and relief. It touched the soul so deeply. I had never experienced such a feeling of completion, after so many relationships and indulgences; I finally got the message, 'don't mess with this energy'. For me, sexual energy had been connected to dependency and expectations that, if they are not met, led to conflict in the form of power-games and manipulation. I had been a player, and had been played for long enough and it was time to jump out of the game, to transcend that base energy and to channel that drive into something worthwhile and productive, rather than continuing to destroy myself and others.

It was time to 'serve' others, not to take, take, take. Now was my time to start giving; giving back to the world all that I had taken. It was like a flash of understanding. That this was finally the last time in the cycle. 'Liberated' is the word I would use to explain the feeling of letting go of lust, which had governed my life for decades. Freedom, dignity and self-respect became my reward and a new chance, a fresh start. A feeling of innocence filled my life with new meaning and a new direction.

Dreams and sanskars still influence me every now and again, but the trick is not to give them any energy and not to put them into action even if thoughts come, and they do. This is something I continue to check and work on constantly. It really does take constant attention in every interaction to re-programme the subconscious mind and the unconscious mind in order to purify our sanskars and dreams. I have the determined thought and feeling that I will be victorious over this most deceptive of vices in the end.

Meditation in Action

It's easy to get lost in the activities of the day, and for the day to be finished and over before you know it. So taking a bit of 'time-out' every now and then to reflect or meditate is my way of keeping aware and in touch with exactly who I am and how I am engaging with the world and those around me.

"Am I being soul conscious in this very moment?" is my checking method and I repeat it in my mind regularly. To do this, I observe myself between activities or tasks that need to be completed, and I check myself for awareness throughout the day, detaching from the role that I am playing, just for a few seconds. This is all it takes to keep the switch of soul consciousness on. I see myself as a being of light and, in that consciousness, let go and fly, completely free. In my mind's eye, I reach the Home of Light and peace and silence, recharge with energy and then come back into the here and now. Once connected to my eternal nature, that of peace and happiness, I go into any actions that need to be performed.

This 'break' or space is very useful, as I find that tension and stress dissolve and I can be much more focused and productive in whatever it is that I am doing. It's very practical. Nobody even needs to know that I am practising this. It only takes a few seconds. However, the benefits are enormous. It builds up my awareness and it brings lightness and a sense of freedom, even if I am involved in an ordinary task, such as just before driving the bus.

It is a safety net, as I become very present in each moment and not distracted in the way I used to be. Each action now has value and is performed as part of the overall game of life. My frustration and irritation is reduced and even the most tedious jobs become a method to advance, increase my stage of self-awareness and achieve new, internal spiritual goals.

The mind is kept busy in this consciousness and is less likely to cause mischief, so I become less anxious and upset by small things. This reduces tension and stress. Interactions with others become positive and there is less chance of needlessly wasting my precious energy. This way of living is one of the greatest lessons that I have learnt. It is the gift that I was given to help me to stay in the now. Meditation is a simple activity to remain involved in; yet it has changed my entire attitude towards living. It gives me reason to get out of bed in the morning!

Now every moment is used in a worthwhile way. My attitude now (which is the platform that I build my thoughts on) has moved from being either 'at work or not at work' (this would influence my responses and interactions with others) to being a complete lifestyle of positive experience full of interest, opportunity, energy and yoga.

Meditation is a tool for the soul to reach its highest potential and so have a positive and beneficial impact on the world around it. It is the energy of transformation and we can reform ourselves through it. "As I change, the world around me changes."

By connecting to the eternal part of me, that of spiritual light which can never be destroyed, or created for that matter, I am able to see through my 'third eye' of awareness. I am able to know myself and my original and eternal qualities. These are of love, peace, happiness, wisdom and purity. All of which together make up Power. The power of I, the soul. This is very much our truth. It's just that we have forgotten it.

Now, as I reflect on this aspect of myself and focus my attention and concentration, it becomes like a 'laser', able to cut through situations and find the truth and so find what is of benefit to me and what isn't. This is the Power to Discern.

The sun shining is a good example.

The sun is always shining. There may be clouds blocking the rays of light, but behind them you can find the sun and its rays of light and heat are everywhere. It's when we can focus that energy from the sun that we can use it. If we use a lens to collect the light and direct it, it becomes concentrated and can be used to transform or cut through impurities. It can burn away rubbish.

Our consciousness is the same. Whatever we focus our attention on will expand, it will get bigger. Keep thinking about a problem and the problem will get worse as well as using up our energy. Focus on a positive solution to that problem and that positivity will increase.

In meditation it is as though I am increasing my 'treasures' that were hidden in the corners of my being. Bringing these qualities into the centre of my awareness and giving them energy or power, they begin to fill me up. As I become full, all the negativity and sadness decreases. I don't have to chase it away; it just gets replaced with these expanding positive energies.

The environment around me becomes influenced by these qualities and the atmosphere in the place that I find myself begins to become transformed, becoming full of positive energy. It's subtle, but very powerful. This is the effect that the power of positive thinking has on the vibration of the atmosphere. As this energy starts to overlap, it becomes richer and more and more tangible. Then it starts to influence people's attitudes in a very subtle way. It's amazing and so simple when we work from the inside, out.

An example of this phenomenon is distance healing, where a group of people focus on someone who is ill and send positive energy to that one collectively, whilst in a different location. This energy is received on some level and can help with recovery from illness. Sending light and love (positive thoughts) to the whole world while in meditation is a common practice for many spiritual people. It may seem like imagination, but its thoughts that create, and when 'conscious beings', who understand this spiritual law, practise this, miracles can happen.

The Berlin Wall is a physical example of this. It took a huge amount of conscious effort to remove this symbolic dividing wall between East and West. But it was the 'collective energy' of many, both close and distant, that together made it happen.

'Creative visualisation' or 'cosmic ordering' is another practice many people use to create their future. They see a positive situation or outcome in their minds, then regularly give energy to it and 'manifest' that occurrence to happen. Some people are remarkably good at this and use it to live their lives.

Capacity

There is an extra element that we now have to take into consideration. As a soul, I have a certain capacity. This is the volume or the amount of power that I can contain. Each soul has its own part recorded within it and no one soul is any better or worse than any other. They are just different and have different roles to play, depending on their specialities and qualities. Each soul is eternal and unique, and has its own perfect set of qualities, and it's this mixture that makes us all unique.

This is what makes the play so wonderful and diverse. After all, it would be a bit dull if everyone were the same, don't you think?

A glass that is full of water can only hold that much water. This is its capacity. Some glasses are small and some are large, some glasses are as big as a swimming pool, some are as big as an oil-super-tanker, if you see where I am coming from. This capacity is how much water each one can hold. If you place this glass, no matter what size it is, under a tap of water, it will, once full, overflow. As it overflows, the water will flood the area around the glass.

This is the same way we can flood the area around us with positive energy or light when we connect to the Source. Not the source of water as in this case, but the

Source of love, peace, happiness, wisdom and purity, which all together equals Power. This is the aim of meditation. It is to link the mind and intellect to that 'Divine' source of power, The Supreme Soul. For this, I need to stretch my mind and intellect upwards, to the Source of all positive energy.

You can call this Source anything you like - the Divine, the Lord, God, Allah, the Father, Shiva, the Holy Spirit. I used to call it the Universe, but really this energy is outside of the physical Universe, so now I call it the Supreme Soul. This is the non-physical 'Living Energy Source' that is infinite and can never run out. An unlimited positive energy, which is always giving and, guess what? It's free, absolutely free. So you can't lose anything by trying it for yourself.

The only questions are, "How much do I want? "What priority am I going to give this in my life?" and "How serious am I about improving my life and the lives of others?"

We spend so much of our time looking after the body and pampering it.

How much time do we give to our inner self, the soul?

Maybe this is the reason why the world is so out of balance? We've been looking after the bus (body) thinking that it's me and forgetting to feed the driver (soul), so the driver has become a bit withered and weak!

As with the glass being filled with water, the soul is filled with positive qualities by connecting to this unending stream of light or energy, through the method of meditation. This stream is reaching this planet from the Supreme Soul, who resides outside of the physical Universe in the Home of Light, which is also our Original Home of Light. I only need to give myself the time and space and silence to focus and concentrate, and link to the Stream which is arriving from this Ocean, and I can overflow.

It's easy. Just begin to visualise an infinitely powerful point of gentle light, sending a stream of power in your direction in order to fill you up with all positive qualities.

This was exactly what was happening in the 'Laughing and Crying' experience that I had in those early days of practising meditation. Meditation is the most powerful of tools. What do you think?

It's worth a try?

Go on, treat yourself!

Knowledge

"Godly spiritual knowledge is given by God-Father Shiva, the Supreme Soul, Father of all souls at this transformational time period between the old world and the new world."

This is what I was told at one point towards the end of my spiritual journey, but what on earth does it mean?

Well, my understanding is that the world is in a bit of a state at the moment. Everything seems to be out of balance and out of shape. Whether it's the individual or the family, the community or the work place, the economy or the country, and the entire globe, including the animal kingdom and nature, all seems to be disharmonic and unstable. Everything seems to have reached its extreme and needs to change, as the current way of living is non-sustainable and destructive. The Earth is almost beyond repair due to the negative tendencies of mankind. These tendencies were firstly created within our minds.

It will take a switch of consciousness to recover from this extreme. It seems that we have forgotten our morals, values, virtues, qualities and all respect for life and all that is alive, including our planet, the Earth. This forgetfulness is not our fault. It is also part of this 'Great Drama' that we call life, on this 'Great Stage' that we call the Earth.

As a spiritual being, from an eternal point of view, through the eyes of soul consciousness, we can remain an observer. We can be 'detached observers' of each scene or 'guests' within this unlimited playground. From this awareness, we can see that it will take a very powerful energy to change the direction of our thinking - an energy that is outside of this closed system that we call the physical Universe. A Being who is Living Light is needed, in order to wake us up from this deep sleep of ignorance that we have fallen into simply due to forgetting who we are. This is a Being who is only benevolent and is full of endless love and truth. A Being who never forgets and can never reduce in power, as that Being doesn't enter into the account of birth and death and so is not subject to entropy, but is able to enter into the system in order to give the answers to all the problems of the world.

And this switch is soul consciousness. This is the overall 'solution' because, as it is practised, there is natural respect for everyone and everything.

If we are souls in bodies, then it makes sense that there could be a Supreme Soul, one that guides and supports as a Father/Mother of souls or Spiritual Parent. This 'Re-Creator' uses His unlimited power to transform the old broken world and create a renewed world of happiness. For this transformation from old to new, there needs to be some sort of 'mechanism'. Surely it can't be done though divine inspiration or by mere human beings?

Also, how can we know or believe that this is true?

Perhaps the only way we can be sure of the existence of such a Being is for that Energy to personally come Herself. Well it's not a He or a She, and it's definitely not an It. After all, this is not a bodily being that we are talking about, but a Being of pure living light.

In many beliefs, the Father has been remembered and my feeling is that this is the highest Father; you could say the Father of all fathers or the perfect Father. He is unconditionally loving and positive in every way. This One is the 'Ocean of Knowledge' and the 'Bestower of Happiness', the Truth. He is also the Mother, Teacher, the Guide and the Friend. It's like having all the relationships that we have in a bodily sense rolled into one perfect relationship between the soul and the Supreme Soul, with nothing to get in the way.

Can you imagine how nice that would be? He needs nothing from us, but is only giving. The feeling is also that He comes from His home, or, you could say the Soul World, which is a world of silence and stillness and is the Original Home of all souls. Through meditation, we can experience that place of rest and be with the Divine.

He comes from this Home and, through an instrument human being already here, He is able to give His own introduction as the Benefactor of all souls. Some of the knowledge that He gives is that of reminding us who we are, where we came from and where we are going. These were the very questions that had been bugging me for a very long time.

The part of these teachings that interests me most is that we are now at the junction, or confluence, between our old reality and a new one, and that we are about to return home to this Soul World. In order to do this, we will have to clean up our act and become pure, pure light - the make-up of the soul-self. Our true Home is a world without impurity, a world of only golden light. It's the place of rest.

Once we return home, the Earth can then be renewed and cleaned though the five elements, water, fire, air, earth and ether. This seems to make sense to me. It's as if the 'world clock' needs to be reset and this Divine Light is the catalyst to instigate it. This renewal will bring the balance back and provide a heaven-like place on Earth for souls to return to. A place in which to continue playing their parts, in their new costumes, in happiness, free from the accumulation of negativity, which is the state that today's world has fallen to.

If you look around, it almost feels like 'Hell on Earth' in these unstable times. Whether it is on a physical, mental or spiritual level, we are all suffering to some degree. It may be emotionally, financially or health wise, no-one is free or exempt from this pain.

His message is, *"Consider yourself to be a soul and remember Me."*

It's as if just by remembering the Being of Pure Light, we begin to heal ourselves on every level. We have nothing to lose by giving it a try and everything to lose if we don't. So it's worth a go. I have never come across a method that works any better than this simple one.

Attachment

The definition of attachment in this context is that it is a form of 'dependency'.

When I am dependent on someone or something and it is then taken away from me, I feel sad or even feel hurt. (Similar to when a child has his toys taken away from him and he begins to cry.) This sadness in adults can lead to depression and, in its extreme, hopelessness or even suicide. Suicide is not the answer to becoming free from problems. When observed from a spiritual perspective, it is a way of increasing my problems. This refers to the karmic account that is created by taking one's own life. Once reincarnated into another human experience, any outstanding business or account that the soul needs to play out then continues to be settled. Ending the body that 'I', the soul, am responsible for is a way of adding to my account of wrong actions and so this will also need to be rebalanced next time around.

Attachment is subtle.

Sometimes we don't even realise that we are attached to someone or something. The tell-tale signs are that I feel pain or anger if that person or thing is taken away from me or is no longer available.

A big test for any parent is to see their children leave home. This 'allowing' or ability to let go, can be cultivated over time, with preparation, for their departure and with acceptance that the child has to become independent and needs to discover the world for herself.

But what if the departure is sudden, for any number of reasons? What if we are talking about death?

We can begin to deal with the loss of loved ones through the vision of soul consciousness, or seeing another as a fellow soul on his journey through life who doesn't actually belong to me but is playing his own unique part as my companion or co-actor. In this way, I can be a trustee or guest within this physical world and know that nothing is mine. I only happen to be looking after it, or them, for a temporary period of time while it is my role or responsibility. This attitude is very freeing.

With this awareness, I can see that I don't actually own anything. I am simply using it in order to experience, learn and interact on this physical plane.

Attachment can destroy my life and the life of others, as I can become possessive, trying to control and manipulate. I cannot ever be 'truly loving' if I am attached. This is because I am be holding on too tightly.

Love lets go, fear holds on.

Putting a full stop to the past enables me to remain in the present moment and to enjoy the unlimited possibilities of now and to create a positive future.

Animals and Nature

In the end, we will need to stop worrying about the environment and nature, and simply live in accordance with the natural laws of respect and regard. Soul conscious eyesight allows us to see what is beneficial to all, whether human, animal or mineral. Harmony can then be restored effortlessly. It's easy.

My understanding of the animal kingdom is that each animal, no matter how big or small, whether an elephant or an ant, has a soul. No, it *is* a soul in its own costume or body. Individual and collective awareness is played out in groups of animals, as indeed it is with humans. A hive of bees operates in an organised manner from queen to worker, as do clans, tribes and communities of people from president to pauper.

Also, souls stay in their own species. So the soul of a cat always returns to a cat body and the soul of a peacock always has a peacock costume. There is no transmigration. Human souls are the same; they always inhabit a human body. However, the human soul has more awareness than animals, usually!

Perhaps any living thing has some sort of spirit or soul, including trees, plants and vegetation, although it may not have self-awareness within it. Plants can affect our consciousness if we ingest them, but maybe their 'life' is connected to their own programme or programming and they have their own 'department'.

The human soul and its vibration, whether high or low, affects the plant world and the animal kingdom. Therefore, when man's consciousness and lifestyle were elevated, plants and animals were also elevated. As man's awareness became degraded over time due to entropy, so animals and plants reflected this and followed suit, as did nature.

In a very general way, human consciousness is the 'indicator' as well as the 'regulator' of its surroundings. It influences matter itself. 'Quantum science' is now proving this. As human consciousness reduces due to the actions that we perform over time, all other 'systems' become a reflection of that level. The Earth was once a paradise and you could say, Heaven, a Garden of Eden. Because of our actions over a period of time, it has been reduced to its present level. Even in its reduction, there is such beauty in the world.

Can you possibly imagine how it once was in its highest form, when it was on full power? When it was full of light and only positive energy?

I have, through my travels as a young man, been lucky enough to witness some amazing events on this Earth: such as a pod of over 500 dolphins intersecting the path of the ship on which I travelled. They were jumping and playing, surrounding the vessel in all directions during one journey in Alaskan waters some years ago.

On the same trip, I also saw huge whales leaping into the air, performing tricks while feeding on their favourite food, plankton.

I have enjoyed majestic elephant rides in the jungles of Thailand, and handled boa constrictor snakes, green tree frogs and a giant praying mantis in Australia.

I have gazed at phosphorus in the ocean as it shimmered in the moonlight around tropical islands like nature's neon waves and meteor showers cutting strips in the night sky, not dissimilar to water droplets running down a pane of glass.

I have been fascinated by the beauty of the Aurora Borealis (the Northern Lights), looking as if the entire sky was on fire with dancing flames of red and orange.

I have witnessed glaciers of deep blue compressed ice as they shed their faces, before sliding into the ocean with thunderous explosive power.

I have marvelled at the huge waterfalls cascading from all directions at Niagara and explored snow-topped peaks during adventures in the Himalayas; first jungle, then arid barren terrain, then a frozen landscape of ice and deep snow drifts at great altitude.

I stood in astonishment at the magnificent tropical rainforests of Queensland, Australia, and at the vast deserts at Uluru. I have explored the marine Paradise world of the Great Barrier Reef, swimming amongst thousands of multi-coloured fish, and even sharks, in a coral undersea garden teaming with sea-life of every variety.

I visited great tea plantations in India, played on the tropical Islands of the Caribbean, and wondered at the Grand Canyon and the lost Indonesian temples such as Borobudur.

My mind has boggled with fascination at the Panama Canal, that joins the Atlantic Ocean to the Pacific Ocean, a man-made piece of genius.

The mountains of Europe, with its glaciers and scenery, humbled me.

This planet has such a variety of vegetation, temperature and humidity. Its culture and lifestyles are so diverse. These are just some of the riches, which I have been fortunate enough to experience during this lifetime. Yet, within all this beauty and wonder, there is so much pain, suffering and degradation. Negativity is rife, and violence and horror are the very fabric of reality. The foundation is greed, anger and desire, as well as abuse. Ego has become King and attachment is Queen. The world is at its all-time low right now. The population is high and resources, such as food and clean water, are low. These are then shared out in a disproportionate way, with no regard for the poor.

It is said that, "You can judge the level of a civilisation by its lowest member." Do you think that our global society is civilised?

Can you see the way we treat each other in the body-conscious awareness that we think is normal? There is zero respect for others, nature and even for ourselves. Soul consciousness instantly repairs our approach to life in a second, in a natural way, restoring both balance and harmony. It reconstructs our values and lifestyles instantly. It transforms not only each individual being, but also it impacts the elements themselves and the nature around us. It is the only hope we have for unity and peace in this world on Earth.

We just have to try it. Then, when enough of us are practising this awareness and a critical mass is reached of souls who are 'awake', which only has to be a small percentage of the population, transformation on a global level will take place.

Entropy

Entropy is the name given to the process that takes place when something starts off in its highest form and loses energy over time, finally reaching its lowest form. This is a scientific concept, which also works on a spiritual level.

The bus is a good example.

When it first goes into service, it is brand new, has the latest registration plate and is the latest and most up-to-date model. It has all the newest technology on board and everything works. There are no scratches or dents to the bodywork, and the engine is clean and smooth running. There are no leaks, no dirt inside or outside of the vehicle. All in all, it is a pleasure to drive and to ride on. The seats are comfortable and clean, the heaters work properly, as does the radio, windscreen wipers and all the lights and lighting.

Now, as it is used to carry people from one place to another, it begins to become a bit tatty. The driver might scrape the paintwork a little every now and then, or even the bumper, or wheel arches, or perhaps make a few dents by mistake. The floor starts to become a little dirty, even if it is cleaned regularly, as does the upholstery on the seats, and the handrails become worn. This is normal, natural, wear and tear. It happens slowly over a period of time.

This is entropy at work.

The bus is becoming a little old and tired, especially after a few years. Time continues to pass and the engine of the bus starts to become less reliable, the lights become damaged and the bodywork starts to look a bit dented. After 10 years, you can see that the technology on the bus is now out of date and the bus starts to look generally dated and old. After another 5 years, the engine reaches a stage of becoming a little unreliable and, on some mornings, it may not even start. With another 5 years, it is past its sell-by date.

So, 25 years have now passed.

The bus is now old and in its lowest form due to entropy. It's had a good life and served many passengers, but there are now two choices.

1) Scrap the bus, as it is costing too much money to maintain.

2) Inject lots of energy into the bus, in the form of spending money on it to restore it back to its former glory.

In this example, the bus is a 'closed system' and the money, which needs to be spent on it to restore it, is an outside form of energy that is not affected by the entropy of the bus. The bus can be restored, but it may not be viable or cost effective. However, this is another matter entirely.

An hourglass is another example, as it is also a closed system.

When we first turn over the egg timer or hourglass, the turning is the energy that makes the sand from the top section start to fall though the small channel down to the bottom of the glass container. Once all the sand has run though, there is no more energy left and it will take more external energy, something which is outside the hourglass system, to start the timer again, i.e. someone to turn the timer over once again.

Our planet, and indeed the whole of the physical universe, is the same. It needs a positive energy or force, which is outside the closed system, to restore balance, light and harmony once again. Everything that we see around us is subject to entropy. Matter, which is stored physical energy, our sun which will one day burn itself out and even the soul which is spiritual energy are all subject to entropy. Each of them moves from its highest form at its beginning, through its middle stage and ends up in its lowest form at its end.

For something to be unaffected by entropy in the system of the physical Universe, it needs to exist outside the physical. The only entity that always resides outside this closed system is the Supreme Soul, God or the Divine - however you want to say it. Because of this, He or She is eternally full, complete and 'lossless'. When the Earth and all of matter reach its lowest form, it will take an unlimited source of energy to recreate it as it once was.

As with the situation of restoring the bus, matter, as well as the soul-self, needs to be injected with energy, but this time not in the form of money, but in the form of positive energy or 'Pure Power'.

So the question is, "At what point of the process of entropy have we reached at this time period in the 21st century? "

My feeling is that entropy has taken its toll on both matter, of which our bodies are made, and every individual soul itself. Everything now needs to be restored or recreated back to its original splendour.

What do you think?

Time

From an early age, we have been taught to think that time is linear and goes in a straight line from one point to another. Somehow this doesn't make sense to me.

Have you ever noticed how just about everything around us works in a cycle?

The seasons go around, spring, summer, autumn, winter. The lunar cycle, as well as day and night, are cyclic. The hours of a clock pass by, going round and repeating. Women's cycles work in monthly time frames.

The water cycle: from rain, to rivers, to the ocean, to clouds, which are then carried to high land on the wind, then fall again as rain, and round and round it goes. Even the cycle of birth and death, reincarnation, goes around.

What about time?

Could that also be cyclic?

It would definitely make sense and many beliefs subscribe to this way of thinking, calling it the wheel of time or the procession of the equinoxes.

The Drama

One way of understanding this game of life is as William Shakespeare said, "All the world's a stage. And all men and women merely players". We are simply playing our parts within this drama, play, film or movie.

A play has a beginning, middle and an end, and within that there are many scenes and a great deal of variety. There is diversity, with actors playing the part of good and bad characters. They play different roles on various sets with different scenery. Each act has the correct backdrop, depending on its requirement. All the actors wear their own costume. There is a story line, with plots and sub-plots threaded throughout the performance. Each actor has her script to read and endeavours to play her part to the best of her ability, trying her best and hoping to receive an award.

In a film, not all the actors play a part at the same time. One may play his part from the beginning of the movie, whereas another has his first scene half way through or even towards the end. All the actors are needed to make the film interesting and complete. There may be happiness in some scenes and sorrow in others. There is laughter and tears; all emotions and experiences are needed to show the contrast of possibilities.

At the end of the play, all the actors come on to the stage before they change out of their costumes and go home. Then according to their part, they take to the stage for the next performance just at the right time. By which time, the stage has been cleared and cleaned, and everything has been put back in its correct position or place in order for the next show to begin.

Maybe *this* play, the Drama of life is about to finish and it's time for us to go home now?

The Eternal Home

This is a nice story, try it on for size and observe what it does to your awareness. You may need to stretch your mind and make your intellect broad and unlimited, but if you are lucky, it might even fit.

We are visitors in this world, travelling, just like the driver of the bus going from place to place, enjoying the ride. We look out of the windows (eyes) and drive the bus (body) using all the appropriate controls. This is a short visit that we are making, and it's for a temporary period of time in order to experience ourselves and know ourselves in the physical world. However, this is not our home, we are guests.

Like a game, or like actors on a stage, we enjoy many parts, with different roles that we 'choose' on some level, according to our actions. We are beings of light, people of light, like non-physical stars, and we originally come here from our 'Home of Light', which you could say is a 'sky beyond a sky', of golden-red bliss, eternally. We are never created and can never be destroyed; we are eternal and live together in a family of stars, in our Home of Light, together with the Supreme Parent of all souls, in silence and stillness. Forever.

Now here's the good bit.

That Home of Light is always ours and we can't ever lose it. But as an extra treat, we decide to leave our home for a short while, just for a visit, and come down in a small space suit (body) onto the Earth. This space suit then grows according to our movements and actions as we play a part and have fun within this drama. Remember, the Earth isn't always out of balance and broken as it is today, but is originally a Paradise, a 'Golden Age'.

Not all souls come down at the same time. They trickle down according to the role that they are to play, just like in a movie. Now once you, the soul, have landed on the earth and entered into your first space suit, the agreement is that you recycle your suit for a new one once that particular role is completed. Then, once settled into your new recycled outfit, you can begin to play another role. You don't go back home until all of your family of stars have arrived to try out this playground together and to have fun, as well as learn about themselves in the physical dimension.

Finally, when everyone has come down from their home in the sky and has enjoyed this amazing, multi-faceted game of interactions, expression and diversity, and the Soul World (home) is empty except for the Supreme Being, it's time to return home. Just before returning, all souls are here together in their costumes, acting out their parts in this 'block-buster, ultra-high-budget movie', on this huge stage that we have named Earth. By this time, most of us have forgotten that we are just visiting and we have begun to take everything far too seriously, thinking that we are our 'space suits' (bodies) and forgetting that we are the drivers sitting inside the costume and that we are separate from that costume.

At this point, the Hero Actor (Supreme Soul) arrives on the stage, borrows a space suit that is already here and fully grown, so as not to be limited by the cycle of birth and death, and wakes all souls up by reminding them, *"Consider yourself to be a soul and remember Me your Father."* This then reminds us all of our home, the land of peace, the sky of golden-red light, from which we came in the first place just to visit. Simple.

Slowly, over the period of 100-years or so, all the actors 'wake up' and remember that they are, in fact, just visiting. Once a critical mass of souls has become 'enlightened', then everyone takes off their space suit and joins the Hero in returning back to their perfect, sweet home of silence, stillness and light, for a well-earned rest and some recuperation.

The stage is then given a good wash, as it has become dirty, fragmented and out of shape. After being cleaned, it is ready, once again, to receive a trickle of actors as they arrive and start once again to play in their costumes in a Paradise-like land of happiness.

How's that?

Nice huh?

This is how I tend to look at the bigger picture. I don't know if it is true, but it sure makes life easier to deal with while we are here. I find it makes things light and, also, I am able to deal with this most delicate of time periods that we are going through as if it were a dance and a game. It sure beats worrying about stuff. After all, they say that 90% of what we worry about never happens anyway! It just wastes our energy. No wonder we always feel tired!!

Don't forget, it is just a story...

...Or is it?

The Angelic Stage

Interestingly, there is also another plane of reality that can be experienced though meditation. It is a Subtle World of movement but no sound. It is a space in between this physical world and the Eternal Home. It's an angelic realm of glowing white light where thought manifests instantaneously. It is a pure world, and it is this 'angelic stage', or experience of it, that is my present aim.

For me, an angel is a subtle being in a body of non-physical light and is beyond the effect of actions. It is this stage of 'being' which comes from attention to soul consciousness over a long period of time.

As the soul becomes cleansed of negativity through meditation and right actions and connection with the Divine, it becomes more and more free from dependency on the physical body and physical world, and it is able to fly in its subtle body of light.

So, imagine if the bus were built around an inflatable bus-shaped balloon, filled with helium. If the driver were to find out that there was another 'Light-Bus' inside the physical body of the bus that was light enough to fly, he could use it to get out of traffic!

Yes, I know, it's a bit of a funny metaphor. I'm just trying to stretch your mind a little to house the idea or concept of an angel, because we don't really believe in them either, do we?

So to take it a step further, while in traffic, the bus remains in the physical on the ground, stuck with no way of moving, but the balloon could travel upwards and over the traffic once the driver is able to work out how to activate or release it. Our Angelic body or light body is like this. It is hiding under the physical body and we don't even know that it is there. It's an energy-body, and we can activate it through practice and release it so being able to fly free from the 'dense' physical world that we find ourselves trapped in each day. This experience of the Angelic stage is a feeling of freedom from the limitations of the physical world. It can be used to visit other dimensions of light and lightness, in order to serve others.

Service to Mankind

Serving others is the most elevated activity I have ever come across. Truly. The feeling of giving or helping others really seems to hit the spot.

Whether showing someone how to do something positive; helping him or her to improve; facilitating or teaching; just giving in some way is all most rewarding. It has become my motivation for life, hence the creation of this book. Whether giving good wishes or co-operation; perhaps sharing knowledge or understanding; uplifting or empowering, happiness is experienced for the self in the now and good karma is accumulated in the bank for the future.

It doesn't have to be money or things that we give, as these are temporary and ordinary. In fact, they are quite limited and can cause a dependency or create attachment. Giving skills, tools, hope, truth and freedom from the mundane and the irrelevant are eternal gifts that are received as light, might, love, peace and happiness.

In the past, I would set my course for happiness and sail on the 'high seas' of uncertainty, caution to the wind, as after all, I never could handle the idea of 'mediocrity'! I always felt that success was guaranteed, so I didn't have to worry about the ending as that would be fine anyway, and the success I was thinking about was that of being HAPPY.

The way that we go about our life is what counts. Kindness, patience and acceptance are useful tools, as is lightness, responsibility and humility. It's our virtues and specialities that become our character and that's what goes with us in the form of personality or sanskars (habits) from birth to birth as we journey though the course of time.

The soul is imprinted with these sanskars. They are the 'impressions' of the actions that we perform the most and are actually recorded within the living light of the soul and carried with us on our journey. They may manifest in our next lifetime as our personality, preferences or habits. They are our unconscious memories that travel with us. It's these sanskars that influence our future existence.

So with this awareness, if we want to take control of not only this lifetime but also the next, we will need to create positive, pure sanskars, which will then travel with us, so creating our future experiences. We need to do this in the Now. You could even say that I am an 'energetic imprint' of my collective sanskars, as they will shape my very future. Therefore, it is in my own interest to act in a way that is positive, as this becomes my 'dharna', my manner or demeanour. When I reinforce this in my every action and interaction, it becomes truly who I am, possibly for many births. Serving others is the best way to rekindle this kind of living.

Acting with virtues makes me powerful, not a power over others, but inner power which also acts as a form of protection from negativity. A pure sense of peace and love are beneficial not only to the self, but to every other being around me. A feeling of non-violence and respect further strengthens my connection with God and so I can become an instrument through which 'great things' will happen.

As a trustee, I can use everything and yet be happily detached and loving to all people, places and possessions, as well as situations. This will enable me to be truly free and a world benefactor at every step.

'Service', helping others, is a means through which to move forward on my path to reach my highest potential.

Holding Court

At the end of each day, I find it useful to review my attitude and activities before sleeping. I do this in my last short meditation of the day and call it holding court.

As the ruler of my physical and subtle organs, I bring them in front of me into my mind's eye to observe their co-operation during the day. This is a chance to check the quality of my thoughts, words and actions for rightness, so I can change them in the future if necessary. This helps to accumulate a 'stock' of good actions in the karmic bank account. Closing any outstanding business or issues is also a good way to sleep tight.

A quick scan through the situations and interactions that have taken place during the day is enough to 'flag-up' any issues that might need attention. Then, heal them with positive and loving thoughts and put them down for the night. If needed, they can then be picked up again in the morning, but generally I find that by the morning there is nothing left to pick back up!

I heard of one person who would hang up all his problems and worries of work each day on the tree outside his house before going into his home and meeting his family. The next morning he would pick them up again off the tree on his way out of the house.

"Funny," he used to think, "When I go to get them in the morning, most of them have disappeared."

Before sleeping, I also check my mind and intellect to see how they performed that day, as to whether they served me or hindered me. I know that they are not who I am, but that they are my co-operative helpers. In this way, I can talk to them and give them a few pointers as to how I want them to work with me the next day. I always speak to them with love, of course.

I also observe my sanskars or habits that may have been triggered that day and make sure that the physical sense organs were obedient and working for me, not against me. Then I hand everything over to God and sleep sweetly, programming my intellect to wake me up in the early morning for some meditation to start the day. I also set two alarm clocks, just in case!

The morning meditation is really the foundation of life. It's the cleanest time to connect to the Divine, as most souls are asleep and peaceful at that time. I find that between 4am and 5am is the best time, when things are most still. Why don't you try it for yourself? I dare you.

For me, the early morning is the time to fill with power and light, and then send it out to the whole world, because the world really needs it right now.

My Experience of God

The word 'God' has become loaded with past prejudgments, experiences, hopes and disappointments. The word can also give the feeling of distance, making God seem a long way away from us.

In the past, wars have been fought in the name of God; today some people blow themselves up, as well as others, in the name of God.

My feeling is that God is the Source of only positive energy. The Source is benevolent and the Remover of Sorrow, the Bestower of Happiness. He is the Ocean of Love and 'all accepting'. She never causes any sorrow. It is our own forgetfulness or illusion, our ignorance of the truth, which causes sorrow. When we think that we are the body, all our problems begin. When we are being soul conscious, we are living in truth.

By understanding that we lose power and direction as we incarnate and then reincarnate, we can see how mistakes are made; how we become weak and negatively charged. Through this negative energy, 'matter' becomes influenced and deteriorates accordingly. The reduction of positive energy is where the sorrow comes from, as does all sadness and pain. It comes not from the Divine, but due to our many desires, wants, greed, as well as anger, attachment and ego of body consciousness.

My experience is that God, the Supreme Soul, is the Supreme Parent of all souls, our Teacher, our Guide and our Friend. He is Knowledge-full and never forgets. She never reduces in power. It is constant.

It is human beings who forget and who begin to identify with the body. We then get lost in our own deception and in a whirlpool of illusion. He 'allows' us to play our parts and do this as we wish with our own free will. She lets us play out all possibilities on this physical plane. Then, when She sees that things have reached their extreme, through our own body consciousness, She comes and gives us the knowledge that we are spirits or souls and that we have just forgotten that we are that.

His message is simple, *"Consider yourself to be a soul and remember Me your Father."* Another interesting point that He makes when he brings His message is, *"Now the play is coming to an end and you have to return home."*

I feel that the Divine Mother, who is always bodiless and pure light, has the form of a non-physical point of light and is constantly giving. She is not everywhere, but Her rays of light are everywhere. He has His Home of Light, which is also our original home, and His rays of love, light and might are everywhere and do reach every being. All we have to do is to connect and recharge with His unlimited, unending power of peace, happiness, love, purity and wisdom.

I have found that meditation is the way I can meet the Father/Mother. It is the method to experience a union with God.

The Alchemist

In the end, it is the Supreme who is the true alchemist who transforms the soul that has become 'iron' and rusty with negativity, into one that is full of virtues. Once the soul has become full of virtues, it is like gold, precious and beyond the tarnish of anything negative.

Through knowledge and understanding, He reforms our self-respect, reminding us that we are just like Him, pure, positive spiritual energy. By focusing on His qualities, there becomes no room for negativity to remain within us. The five main negativities that are removed from within the soul through remembrance of the Father are: -

Desire – the tool that we use either on a subconscious or intentional level to manifest selfishly our thoughts on a material or physical level.

Anger – which comes in all forms, on all levels, internal or external, should always be acknowledged, handled constructively and never suppressed.

Greed – discontentment is the root of greed, like the obsession of more, more, more.

Attachment – is identifying with external objects or roles, which are detached and separate from the true self. It's also the fear of letting go.

Ego – this identification with the body, masks the fear of loss with the idea that 'mine' is better than the rest. Then the defence of this identity can become overwhelming.

These are the acquired weaknesses of the soul over many experiences, circumstances and situations that have damaged or hurt us. The negative acquired weaknesses are then transformed into love, peace, happiness, purity and wisdom through a connection with the Source of all positive qualities. These are our original and eternal qualities; they just need to be activated once again. The Supreme Soul is the catalyst to activate our true nature. She is the true Alchemist.

Try reflecting, contemplating or meditating on the true nature of the human soul and you will see for yourself the help that He gives. When we take one step of courage, God gives a thousand-fold help.

"So what?"

"So what?" I hear you say. And you have every right to think that.

'Imagination...' or just 'a load of old cobblers' (that's English slang for rubbish or garbage) is another way to put it, or perhaps you even used stronger language than that!

If you have read this far, the fact is that something has already happened, something that you cannot change. A wise traveller that I met along the way shared with me, "Once you know, you can't not know," and I think he was right about that. Although it did take me a while to work out what he was talking about!

A seed of new thinking or a fresh concept has been planted - the seed of 'soul consciousness'. It may not grow just yet or it may have already started to sprout. Maybe it's already a huge tree that you are very familiar with and that you have far more understanding of than the few humble experiences that have been given to me.

However it is, "It's all good." It's all about 'timing' you see. When we are ready, the drama, through the Universe, inspires us to awaken. When that fateful leaflet saying 'Learn to Meditate for Free' materialised into my hand, I was standing at the doorway to a new way of life, love and learning. At that moment, I chose to walk through the door and get on to the bus that was travelling in the right direction for me at that time. I am also sure that there have been other similar moments throughout my life that I chose not to get on the bus. I just wasn't quite ready to go that way.

We all have many things to do and acts to play; we have people to meet and places to go. But exactly at the right time, we will be ready for what it is that we need to do, whatever part we are to play. Really there is no right or wrong. How can we know what is right or wrong until the whole game has been played out? It's only at the end that everything makes sense. The rest is merely speculation and each person's opinion or point of view.

In the end, everyone will wake up anyway and the world will set sail in a new direction – the direction of harmony, balance and unity. The only question is, "Do I want to be woken up by 'grandfather-time' and 'mother-nature' or do I want to wake them up?" This is a nice riddle to meditate on, give it a try.

At the end of the day, you could say that through an on-going self-experiment spanning three decades, I have reached the point at which I am now standing. This place tells me that if I want to be happy, which I do, it is in my interest to remain soul conscious as much as I can. Soul consciousness allows me to act in a way that is aligned to my truth. My truth of being eternally a living-light. When I am lit with this awareness, the spark of my conscience will only allow me to perform actions that are for the good of me, others and the entire world. This then becomes the only way I can live my life, there is no room for greed, anger or desire; it simply cannot exist within me when I am in this awareness.

Darkness is the absence of light. Light is not the absence of darkness. To dispel the darkness, just turn on the light, that's all. Soul consciousness lights up the soul on its journey, like the headlights keep the bus on the road at night time. Within light, there is no darkness. It's just a question of the brightness or intensity of that light. Likewise, in the early morning when the driver goes into the bus, the first thing he does is turn on the lights and only from this point can he begin to drive the bus properly.

What do you think will happen if he tries to drive the bus in the dark without the lights on? He will definitely get lost at the very least. Probably he will crash the bus and for sure he will be confused as there will be no clarity during his journey!

Turning the light of awareness on within the soul-self is the best chance we have to navigate this body of ours through life's unexpected twists and turns. How can we even imagine driving the body along with the soul switched off? So remember, don't forget to turn on the light!

The 'darkness of ignorance', being spiritually asleep and in body consciousness, can be dispelled by knowing and constantly remembering who 'I' am. Every now and then, throughout the day, connecting to myself and then to the Supreme will guide me along my route effortlessly. Then I can remain present in the now with all its magic. I won't miss out on what's happening right in this moment through getting lost in the past or the future.

When the driver looks into the mirrors of his bus, what does he see? He sees the past. He sees what is behind him. Yes of course he needs to use his mirrors and to know who and what is around him, but if he is constantly transfixed on what he can see in his mirrors, then he is not looking at the road ahead. This will undoubtedly create an accident! We are the same. Learn from the past, but watch the past for too long and we will crash, so to speak.

Equally, if the driver is looking far ahead on the road, looking into the future, he will miss the scene that he is in now. The images he sees in the distance can and will change by the time he gets to them. Whereas his present position is in real-time and is accurate and happening right now.

Our own desires and expectations for the future can and will change before we get to them. It's the present that is most important. It's not that we shouldn't plan, but more that we don't miss these valuable moments of the now by being mesmerised by the possible future!

'Gadgets' are another trick!

If the driver is always watching his 'sat-nav', then he is not watching the road. Check, "How much time am I focused on my gadgets, iPod or mobile phone?" Am I missing who is standing right in front of me, waiting to give me the 'message of a lifetime' while I am texting someone else!

These have been some of my own experiences. I used to drive my body recklessly. It would give me signals to change my habits in the form of little illnesses, aches, pains and general tiredness, but I would just ignore it and carry on - until I really had no choice but to change. Practice of soul consciousness taught me to love and cherish my bus (body), and to give it regard as my best friend and companion. To send it love letters in the shape of 'good wishes'. Yes, to actually have good thoughts about and for my body.

We are not talking about false pride and ego here, but self-respect and sense of responsibility and honour towards it. I realise that right now this body is the most valuable instrument that I have the fortune of using. Being in it is my chance to help to transform my surroundings, and all those around me, just by 'being' and remaining awake to the self-soul. This is a chance that I cannot let slip or allow to pass me by. I can see that it is this chance that will create my happiness, not only in the present moment, but also, as the law of karma tells me, I will receive a reward in the future as well. This is guaranteed. It's karma (action and its return).

My 'fortune' is the only word I can think of to express the value of the treasures I have uncovered that were hidden within me. Living in body consciousness, I didn't even know they were there, until I began to dig around inside through being soul conscious.

From 'rags to riches'. From 'a beggar to a prince'. From 'a thorn to a flower'. Such is the transformation that has taken place internally, within my awareness.

Virtues can stream out of us naturally and quality is magnified with just a little internal self-development work. Then, through meditation and reflection, many attainments are possible. Our inside and outside are aligned and life flows like a sweet river when it is connected to the 'Ocean of Happiness', to God.

On a practical, physical level, I can see changes that I could not have believed possible, such as the reinvention of kindness, care and empowerment, and a redefinition of perspective, attitude, intention and motivation. An overall vision of brotherhood melts any judgment of age, sex, colour or culture, and unity and equality shape all interactions with sweetness and benevolence. Simplicity now reins over complexity and, "What can I give?" replaces "What can I have?" 'Taking' now makes no sense, as I realise that there truly is 'no such thing as a free lunch'. There is always a price to pay or a return to give.

I am now motivated by wanting to create happiness for myself and others, and by having the pure desire to be an instrument who is open to be used by the highest energy, that of the Divine. This manifests in the form of serving humanity.

As a young person, I always wanted to work for a charity, maybe go to Africa or India, but did not know how that could be possible. My charity now starts at home. Firstly with myself. I give the self-soul the nourishment that it needs, that of spiritual knowledge and time to reflect, through regular meditation. Then once full, I can serve my brothers and sisters through my actions and example.

Over the last 15 years, I have built up the courage and self-respect that I need, and I now facilitate workshops and seminars connected to self-development and meditation. This could never have been achieved when I was operating in body consciousness. I feel that I cannot teach anyone anything, as everything that we need is already inside us. What I can do however is help others to emerge their own truth and to find their path, help others to understand themselves, this drama and God. Then I am fulfilling my duty. This is the consciousness with which I approach teaching. "Enable me to give this soul whatever it needs right now, not what I think it needs," are my thoughts and preparation before meeting any individual or group. I also feel that I am only giving the return of the gift that was so gratefully received by me through Raja Yoga Meditation.

My intention is to continue to give all that I have and to wake up all souls of the world. I say this from my heart and with all my love.

As a volunteer, I use the skills that I have learnt in the past, which have now somehow been purified in order to serve others. The sound and technical experience that I gained from those dark days as a DJ are now used to schedule and produce various meditation programmes. The knowledge of mixing desks, amplifiers, sound systems, microphones, cables and plugs have come in quite handy in recent years.

The interest that I once had in sight-seeing and travel has been transformed, travel is now for service. Through visiting different places I facilitate courses and give talks outlining the benefits of positive thinking and meditation. And I also know that 'as I give, so I shall receive'. Now my time, body, mind and wealth are all used in a worthwhile way. There is not the waste, lack of discernment and focus that used to rule my life. The way is 'clear' and my conscience tells me immediately if something is right or wrong. I just have to listen to it, which I still forget sometimes! The clarity of life is obvious now and often I find that I can read people and situations ahead of time, so being able to avoid misunderstandings and conflicts. All in all, life is sweet.

I still work as a bus driver, only now it's as if the whole world is part of my bus journey. After all, we are all connected, aren't we? I need to steer the bus in the right direction. The journey has to be as safe and as comfortable as possible and I need to pay special attention to my every thought, word and action. I am constantly aware that I am an actor on the world stage and that I am playing a hero role, as we all are, to the best of my ability.

I also realise that I have to maintain my aim, concentration and focus, and remain the example in every situation, as others will copy whatever I do. I need to keep my standards high and to bring others to that level.

This is my responsibility and my duty to my passengers and to mankind in general. Every day is another opportunity to reach my highest potential and to earn my fortune as a world citizen.

Remembering and Forgetting

It seems to me that this game is a game of remembering and forgetting. Both of which are a blessing as well as a curse.

Remembering is a blessing because it deletes negative energy that is stuck within the soul due to any wrong actions, but it does take effort to remember that, "I am a soul," all the time, and, "I am a child of God." Actually, 'effort' is not a favourite word of mine; I prefer the word 'attention'.

Forgetting is a bit annoying, especially after all that 'attention' to remembering in the first place, but the flip-side is that I am very happy indeed that I can't remember all the 'not so good' stuff from past births, like the spears!

Remembering and forgetting is the eternal breath, the in and out of consciousness itself. It is the breath of pure energy moving on its journey through matter, up and down its axis.

This drama is designed so perfectly when we can observe it through the windows of the bus in a detached, yet loving, manner. There is a variety and dynamic that is incomprehensible and unfathomable, but also reassuringly familiar at the same time. After all, "C'est la vie," as they say, "that's life".

Quotes

"I have to maintain my self-respect and give regard to all, young and old, transform myself and also transform others."

Dadi Prakashmani

(Former Head of Brahma Kumaris World Spiritual University)

"You must be the change you want to see."

Mahatma Gandhi

"We must use time wisely and forever realise that the time is always ripe to do right."

Nelson Mandela

Meditation
- the Soul World

This short meditation is a very useful exercise that can help me to let go of the limited concerns of life and connect me to myself as a being of light. Once I have made this connection, I am free to travel safely as a bodiless soul, with the power of my mind, onwards to my Home of Light, the Soul World, and to reunite with our Divine Parent. Here, I can experience peace and stillness. It is this sense of calm that energises the soul, giving it a taste of truth. It is also a place where I can know myself as an eternal being.

Relax, and let go...

Become present, in the now....

Let go of the past, just for a few moments, and let go of the future.... just for a few moments...

This is my time. Time for me, because I am worth it...

I remember the location of where I, the soul, sit within this body...

I am the tiny spark that gives life to this body, the costume that I am sitting in...

I sit on my throne, as the king or queen of my kingdom, at the centre of the forehead, between the eyes, looking out...

Sparkling... sparkling light...

Beginning to slow down my thoughts...

Slowing my thinking...

Creating space...

Space within...

I feed my mind with positive feelings and thoughts of love, peace and happiness...

I allow myself to experience these feelings as I focus my attention...

I am a being of peace... love... happiness...

Becoming light... lighter... lightest... able to float...

Lighter and freer... floating upwards in the flying machine of my mind and intellect... like a magic carpet...

Travelling on the power of thought, I continue to float upwards and outwards.... absolutely free...

Free as a bird in the sky... leaving the weight of the physical body down below... as I glide safely up into the sky... on the wings of concentration and focus...

I focus on my light-body...

My body made of light with light all around, and completely light... floating, upwards...

Past the Moon and Sun, and stars... beyond... and into a subtle, world of angels...

Subtle white light is surrounding me and, gently, lifting me onward... So much silence, with form and movement... but no sound...

Gently onwards, ... free to fly upwards...

Reaching a sky of golden light…

This is a sky beyond a sky… full of golden-red light…

A beautiful golden-red sky of bliss… perfect… blissfulness…

Just a sparkling point of light now. Like I am a tiny diamond; suspended in an ocean of soft, gentle, perfect light…

A perfect sky of blissful, golden, red light…

…Non-physical light…

I am full, complete, and absolutely free and beyond…

Beyond fear and sorrow, beyond anything limited…

Now in the unlimited, with no boundaries, no limitations, no ceiling…

Bodiless…. Weightless… Ageless…

Genderless… Timeless…

I need nothing, I am completely full, safe and secure…

Beyond food, water and even air…

Floating in an ocean of golden-red non-physical light…

Eternal and always… forever…

Finally free, nowhere to go, nothing to do… just my home of rest and light, and safety, a perfect sky… the best sky… my eternal Home of Light…

So much silence… peace… and stillness…

… Always…

In my Home of Light, surrounded by other sparkling stars of light just like me…

Beyond... free... full... and secure...

Always...

So much peace...

Gently floating on the waves of the Ocean of Love... towards the Source...

The Source of all love... peace... happiness... purity... wisdom... and power...

Attracted by a gentle magnetism...

Effortlessly being pulled to the centre of this perfect sky of golden-red blissfulness...

This Divine Energy is gently calling me home... to the One that I had forgotten about...

The Supreme Parent... the Perfect Mother and Father...

My Divine Guide and Teacher is beckoning me back into Her presence... with unconditional love and light...

As I approach the very power source of all positive energies, I recognise this place... recognise this Being...

My perfect Home of Light, my Supreme Parent...

The One I was separated from and became lost from, is calling me home...

Closer and closer to the Source... nearer and nearer...

So much love... so much wisdom...

The ever-pure Divine Mother embraces me in light...

I am home, being held in love...

No more searching...

No more wandering...

Just unconditional acceptance…

Truth… Light… and Might…

I can be in this place for as long as I wish…

Soaking up the rays of all positive qualities…

Recharging my batteries…

Enjoying such happiness…

Reconnected with my Father… my Baba.

This is the Benefactor and I can take as much as I wish from this Unlimited Being… whenever I wish…

When I am ready…

I gently begin my journey back to the physical dimension…

Easily back through the golden-red Home of Light…

Back through the subtle Land of Angels…

Through the physical Universe…

Back to the room and reconnect with the physical body/costume… safely… and calmly…

Only, this time, I remember my Home of Light.

I remember my Divine Supreme Parent and Friend…

I stay awake to who I am…

A sparkling star, a diamond, a soul sitting in this body…

As I hold on to this soul consciousness, I maintain this awareness as I come into actions and interact with other souls in their bodies…

Om shanti (I am a peaceful soul)

ACKNOWLEDGMENTS

I would like to thank my spiritual family the Brahma Kumaris both in the UK and all over the world for your efforts and inspiration in striving for a better world.

Thanks to my family who have always supported me in every way.

To all the co-operative souls that helped bring this book into being, to John, Tricia, Lynn, Judy, Liz, K, Leza and Davina. A special big thanks to Neville for your encouragement and enthusiasm right from the very beginning of this book and help to complete what seemed only like a dream to me. Also thanks for your advice, input and generous Foreword.

Thanks to all the teachers, healers, wise souls, known and unknown contributors to this book for helping me to find my purpose in life and the motivation to live a life with direction and focus.

Thanks to my old friend Pierre, for your support and creation of both the book cover and website.

Thanks to you the reader and hoping that I have been able to make some difference in some small way to your life in a positive way.

Best wishes to you all.

www.eternalpointoflight.com

Made in the USA
Charleston, SC
02 May 2015